The Country Life Book of

DIANA
Princess of Wales

The Country Life Book of
DIANA
Princess of Wales

Lornie Leete-Hodge

Crescent Books

New York

Reprinted 1982

First English edition published by
The Hamlyn Publishing Group Limited
London · New York · Sydney · Toronto
Astronaut House, Feltham, Middlesex, England

ISBN 0-517-37479 X

This 1982 edition is published by Crescent Books
Distributed by Crown Publishers, Inc.
h g f e d c b a

Printed in Italy

Contents

The
Early Years

Park House, on the royal estate of Sandringham in Norfolk, was the birthplace, on a hot July afternoon, of the girl destined to become the wife of the Prince of Wales, and the third lady in the land, at St Paul's Cathedral twenty years later.

Diana Frances, third daughter of the Viscount and Viscountess Althorp, was born at their home on 1 July 1961. The house, which overlooks the park, stands about half a mile from Sandringham House itself. Before her mother and father, who farmed in Norfolk, her mother's parents Lord and Lady Fermoy had lived there.

Lord Fermoy, who was Member of Parliament for King's Lynn for thirteen years, died in 1955, and shortly afterwards Lady Fermoy became Lady-in-Waiting to the Queen Mother, an appointment she still holds. A distinguished pianist, she lives in London and has for many years been closely associated with the King's Lynn Festival.

It was a hundred years since Queen Victoria and Prince Albert purchased the Sandringham estate from the revenues of the Duchy of Cornwall for Prince Edward, Prince of Wales, later King Edward VII.

Park House, Sandringham, the birthplace and childhood home of the Princess of Wales.

The estate includes eight parishes with woodland and farmland, and many houses let to friends of the Royal Family.

Norfolk, renowned for its huge hedgeless fields and its woodlands, makes ideal farming country. A field of ripening corn on a summer's day presents a beautiful expanse of colour that is a delight to behold. This county of contrast and tranquillity, with wide acres of farmland and sleepy little parishes, boasts a great city and the Broads so beloved of holidaymakers. The air is keen and invigorating, and the great estate quickly became a favourite of its royal owners.

In the last hundred or more years it has seen many changes. Sandringham House was remodelled by its first royal owner Edward VII, who added a bowling alley and billiards and smoking rooms so fashionable at that time. Later he changed his ideas and removed his additions, creating the present house.

The Norwich Gates were made in Norwich as a wedding present to Prince Edward and Princess Alexandra and shown at the International Exhibition of 1862. Prince Charles and Lady Diana also received gates for their home at Highgrove as a present, given by the people of Tetbury in Gloucestershire.

King George V spent much of his early life at Sandringham, and York Cottage, on the estate, was his home for years before and after his

Sandringham House, 1952. The lighted window is of the upstairs sitting-room of the Queen and Princess Margaret after the death of King George VI.

Overleaf: Sandringham House showing one of the lakes.

7

accession to the throne. He introduced the royal pigeons, many of which saw active service in the Second World War, and the show dogs now bred on the estate. Many of the royal dogs are buried in the grounds. Sandringham was the place he loved more than anywhere else in the world. The 'Squire of Sandringham', as he was affectionately known, liked all clocks in the house to be half an hour fast – 'Sandringham time'. It was from his beloved Sandringham that King George V made his first Christmas radio broadcast, and from here too his granddaughter the Queen made her first televised broadcast in the series that is now so much part of the Christmas celebrations.

King George VI was born at Sandringham and baptized at the church of St Mary Magdalene. There he also lay in state, guarded by estate workers, after his death in 1952.

This 'country' home of the Royal Family is a place of contrast, for its twenty thousand acres are carefully farmed, and the grounds afford excellent shooting in the season. The Royal Family are able to enjoy a few

Below: A royal shooting party at Sandringham in 1908.

Right: Princess Elizabeth and Princess Margaret on the platform of a combine harvester on the royal farm at Sandringham in 1943.

Opposite page: Estate workers guarding the body of King George VI in Sandringham church.

The main drawing room at Sandringham House.

weeks of country pursuits, usually at the beginning of each year, though they frequently visit the royal kennels where dogs are trained and bred, and the two studs at Sandringham where the Queen's racehorses are stabled. Her great-grandfather King Edward VII was also a very successful owner, winning the Derby and other races with Persimmon, a race which has so far eluded the Queen. Doublet, the event horse on which Princess Anne won the European Championships, was bred here.

A great deal of renovation and alteration to Sandringham has been carried out during Queen Elizabeth's reign. In Jubilee year, 1977, the old stable block became a museum which was opened to the public. The proceeds go to charity and towards the upkeep of the house and grounds. Produce from the estate goes to Buckingham Palace and other royal residences.

From its early days as a royal home, Sandringham has been a happy place where Kings and Queens entertained their friends. Those who live on the estate are also personal friends of the Royal Family.

Left: The fifth Earl Spencer.

Above: The second Earl Spencer.

Left: The tomb of Sir John and Lady Isabella Spencer, 1522, at St Mary Brington.

13

The House of Commons in 1833. The third and fourth Earls Spencer are in the crowd of MPs.

Lord Spencer, father of Lady Diana, had been Equerry first to King George VI and then to the Queen who, with the Duke of Edinburgh, attended his marriage to the Hon. Frances Roche at Westminster Abbey in 1954. The bridegroom had earlier accompanied the Queen and the Duke of Edinburgh on their Commonwealth Tour of 1953-54. His mother was also a member of the Royal Household, being a Lady of the Bedchamber to the Queen Mother from 1937 until her death in 1972.

Lady Diana's parents moved into Park House after their marriage, and it was the family home until Lord Althorp succeeded his father Earl Spencer in 1975 and inherited the family seat at Althorp, Northampton.

In due time Diana Frances Spencer was christened at the church of St Mary Magdalene on the estate. She was called Frances after her mother.

Sandringham church, as it is known, was extensively restored in 1857 and later enriched with gifts, many of them from members of the Royal Family. King Edward VII gave the organ, King George V the nave roof, and his son King George VI the folding lectern. The American Rodman Wanamaker was also a generous benefactor, and his gifts include the solid silver altar and reredos presented to Queen Alexandra in 1911, the jewelled bible and the processional crosses to commemorate those from the estate who fell in the two world wars.

The church is rich in memorials to the Royal Family, and the marble font in which King George VI and Diana Frances Spencer were baptized was another gift from King Edward VII. A brass cross is set into the floor of the chancel where the coffins of members of the Royal Family rested before being taken to Windsor for burial. There is a tradition that no one may walk on it. When the Royal Family are in residence at Sandringham,

14

Left: A pageant at Althorp with the seventh Earl Spencer as his ancestor the first Lord Spencer, and the present Earl as a Court page.

Above: The seventh Earl and Countess Spencer walking with their son, the present Earl, at the 4 June celebrations at Eton in 1937.

Left: The lobby of the House of Commons, from a Vanity Fair cartoon. The sixth Earl Spencer is third from the right.

Below: The Queen holding an investiture in Auckland while on tour in 1954. Earl Spencer was in attendance as Equerry.

Above: The Princess of Wales's father and mother pictured just before their wedding in 1954.

they worship regularly at the church, and the sight of them walking back to the house through the grounds after morning service is a familiar one on television screens in January every year.

For the Spencer family friendship with royalty is nothing new. The Princess of Wales can trace her ancestry back to Geoffrey le Despencer, Justiciar to Edward II, and members of the family have seldom been far from the Court and public life. For centuries they have been soldiers, merchants, naval officers, politicians and, between times, farmers on a grand scale. John Spencer, knighted by Henry VIII, had bought Althorp with the wealth of generations of sheep farmers, and Sir Robert (fifth of the family to be knighted) owned 19,000 sheep and was reckoned the richest man in England at the time of James I.

Sir Robert was made the first Baron Spencer by Queen Elizabeth, who stayed at Althorp in 1603 where she watched a masque by Ben Jonson. His grandson Henry declared for the King in the Civil War, lent him a small fortune, it is said, and was made Earl of Sunderland by his sovereign. His

16

son Robert, the second Earl, succeeded in being chief adviser not only to Charles II and James II but also to William III. He was a considerable patron of the arts and collected furniture and paintings from all over Europe. His son Charles married Lady Anne Churchill, daughter of the first Duke of Marlborough and the formidable Sarah, from whom the family inherited a large fortune.

It was this wealth that enabled the Spencer family to indulge their taste for the arts and to build up their famous collection of art treasures. But they did not desert politics: the second Earl Spencer was First Lord of the Admiralty at the time of Trafalgar, and the third Earl was a Chancellor of the Exchequer and declined the Premiership, preferring to occupy himself with his first love, farming.

The fourth, fifth and sixth Earls all held high offices of state, and Lady Cynthia Spencer, wife of the seventh Earl and Lady Diana's grandmother, was a Lady of the Bedchamber to the Queen Mother. So from her birth Lady Diana was surrounded by a family accustomed to the idea of close relations with royalty and to a tradition of service to the Sovereign.

Lady Diana grew up at Park House with her two elder sisters, Lady Sarah, born in 1955, and Lady Jane in 1957. A son, John, died in 1960, the year of his birth, and Charles, now Viscount Althorp, to whom the Queen was godmother, was born in 1964, the same year as Prince Edward.

Viscount Althorp and his bride, the former Hon. Frances Roche, at Westminster Abbey. At eighteen she was the youngest bride in the Abbey for fifty years.

Above: One-year-old Lady Diana at her home, Park House.

Their father, the eighth Earl Spencer, was born in 1926 and was a godson of Queen Mary and the Duke of Windsor. He was educated at Eton and Sandhurst, and during the Second World War served in the Royal Scots Greys.

As Equerry to King George VI and the Queen, he was often a guest at Balmoral where he enjoyed shooting with Prince Philip, as he also did at Sandringham. He was acting Master of the Royal Household when he married the Hon. Frances Roche, daughter of Lord and Lady Fermoy, at Westminster Abbey on 1 June 1954. The Queen, the Queen Mother, Princess Margaret and Princess Alexandra were among those present, and it was one of the Society events of that year. Some seven hundred guests attended the reception at St James's Palace.

The Spencer children played and grew up with the royal children, so naturally were all great friends. The Spencers' swimming pool was a big attraction!

Lady Diana's first governess was Gertrude Allen, who also taught her mother as a child and remembered her as a happy child. She recalls her days at Park House as a 'good time in my life'. The youngest daughter loved the family pets, especially the small ones, and, above all, babies. From a very early age she showed her love for and innate affinity with children of all ages. She soon became used to seeing the Royal Family regularly and, most important, informally, and her own upbringing fitted her to be at home with anyone, like Kipling's hero who could 'walk with Kings – nor lose the common touch'.

Opposite page: The baby Lady Diana in her pram at Park House.

19

Viscountess Althorp holding the young Lady Diana in her arms.

In 1968, at the age of seven, Lady Diana became a day pupil at Silfield School in King's Lynn, staying for two years until, in 1970, she went as a boarder to Riddlesworth Hall, a preparatory school near Diss in Norfolk.

The year 1969 was a significant one for her. It was when her parents became divorced, and Lady Althorp married Mr Peter Shand Kydd. The children remained with their father, but visited their mother often. Life went on at Park House with birthdays as special highlights. On Lady Diana's seventh anniversary her father hired a camel called Bert, and she and her brother and friends had a wonderful time playing 'Lawrence of Arabia' and having rides in the grounds of their home.

On Lady Diana's birthday in that same year Prince Charles, who was one day to be her husband, was invested as Prince of Wales at Caernarvon Castle. In 1969 the Prince wrote a children's story *The Old Man of Lochnagar* for his younger brothers and gave a copy to the eight-year-old Lady Diana. It was published in 1980 illustrated by Sir Hugh Casson and has now been recorded on cassette by Peter Ustinov with background music. Profits on sales, as with the book, go to the Prince of Wales Charities Trust.

A drawing of Lady Diana by the late Madame Pawlikowska in 1965.

Lady Diana and her brother, now Viscount Althorp, a former Page of Honour to the Queen, taken in 1965.

21

At her preparatory school Lady Diana enjoyed sports, especially swimming, but is particularly remembered for her care of the younger children. Unhappily, she had a bad fall while riding and broke her arm – and so does not wholly share the Royal Family's love of horses.

In the holidays the children spent much time with their mother who was now living on a sheep farm on the Isle of Seil in Argyllshire, which afforded endless possibilities for the delight of the family. The island also had the great attraction of an open-air life of boating, fishing and swimming – much as the Royal Family enjoy at Balmoral on Deeside.

At twelve Lady Diana became a pupil at West Heath School, near Sevenoaks in Kent. The school, which was founded in 1865, takes 130 boarders and a few day pupils. Standing in its own extensive grounds, it is well equipped for education as well as recreation. The last Princess of Wales, later Queen Mary, was one of its pupils, so it already had royal connections when Lady Diana arrived. The pupils pursued a variety of activities said to develop 'character', and Lady Diana enjoyed music and dancing. She wanted at one time to become a ballet dancer until she grew too tall. It was at West Heath that Lady Diana met one of her closest friends, Carolyn Pride, who later became one of her flatmates at Coleherne Court in London. Lady Diana left West Heath in Jubilee year and was given an award for service, something only presented to outstanding pupils. While there she often helped in a centre for handicapped children, and she also did shopping and domestic chores for an old lady.

But another event of great significance also took place in 1977. During her last term at the school, in November, she went home to Althorp for a

Right: A young Lady Diana with a furry friend.

Below: A camel ride provides a seventh birthday treat for Lady Diana, with a steadying hand from her father.

Bottom: A Spencer family group taken at the golden wedding anniversary of Lady Diana's grandparents in 1969. She is seen on the left of the front row.

Right: A pensive Lady Diana on the Isle of Uist, Scotland, in 1974.

Above: Lady Diana on holiday at Itchenor, Sussex, in 1970.

weekend. The Prince of Wales was her father's guest on a shoot, and her eldest sister Lady Sarah introduced her sixteen-year-old sister to the Prince, as she herself put it, 'in a field'.

Lady Diana's life changed in 1975 when her grandfather, the seventh Earl Spencer, died, and her father became the eighth Earl. The family moved out of Park House and took up residence at Althorp in Northamptonshire. Park House has remained empty ever since, a place of memories and the echoes of childhood.

Althorp's original building of red brick was put up by Sir John Spencer in the early sixteenth century and surrounded by a moat. Alterations have been made to the size and shape of the rooms over the years, and in 1786 Henry Holland was asked by the second Earl Spencer to remodel the

Left: The dormitory at West Heath where Lady Diana slept.

Above: West Heath School where Lady Diana was a boarder.

house and grounds. The moat was filled in and the gardens and park were improved with the help of Samuel Lapidge, chief assistant to the renowned Capability Brown. The present gardens, designed by W. M. Teulon, date from the 1860s. Beyond the lake there is a temple which came from Admiralty House in London and was bought for £3 by the fifth Earl Spencer, First Lord of the Admiralty.

The house contains one of the finest private art collections in Europe, which has much of interest, including items that once belonged to the first Duke of Marlborough. There are some Roman marble figures rescued from the River Tiber and given to the Duke by his brother, as well as a Chinese red lacquer screen presented to him by Leopold I, Archduke of Austria, which he used on his military campaigns. There are also treasures

25

which once belonged to the ill-fated Queen Marie-Antoinette of France. Amongst the furniture is a set of mahogany chairs decorated with the family coat of arms, but left without upholstery so that any unexpected visitors could sit on them in their outdoor clothing.

The famous art collection contains many paintings by Thomas Gainsborough and by Sir Joshua Reynolds, who in 1768 became the first President of the newly founded Royal Academy. In the Picture Gallery, which is some 115 ft (35 m) long, hang portraits of each generation of the family since the time of Elizabeth I, when the gallery was used by the household and their guests for walks on wet days. Since then it has been the setting for presentations and banquets, and was the scene of a glittering reception for King William III in 1695.

Althorp is a rich treasure house of history, a record of the service given to their country by the Spencer family. The Oak Room provides romance, for the first Earl Spencer was secretly married there by his former tutor during a ball held in the rooms below. King William's Room was the State bedroom at the time of the second Earl of Sunderland, and in 1695 King William of Orange slept here, in a bed covered with olive damask and surmounted by four plumes of ostrich feathers. The blue and white tulip vases on the chimneypiece are from Delft in Holland and date from King William's reign. Queen Mary's Room has a royal connection from the twentieth century: it was used by King George V and Queen Mary when they visited Althorp in 1913. The chimneypiece is by Robert

Prince Charles with Lady Sarah Spencer at a polo match at Windsor.

Adam, and the tapestry chair covers were worked by the seventh Earl Spencer, father of the present Earl, who was an expert needleman. He was Chairman of the Executive Committee of the Royal School of Needlework and said he found embroidery the 'finest relaxation he knew'. Many of the chairs at Althorp bear witness to his skill.

For all its grandeur and magnificence, Althorp is a much loved family home, where the family live and work to preserve their heritage. The present Earl is often seen at work on many aspects of his estate, and his heir Charles acts as guide to visitors during his holidays.

In 1976 Earl Spencer married his second wife Raine, formerly the Countess of Dartmouth, and daughter of the novelist Barbara Cartland.

Lady Diana Spencer was then sixteen and left West Heath School in Kent to go to the Institut Alpin, a finishing school at Videmanette near Gstaad in Switzerland. During her time there, her sister Lady Sarah spent a holiday skiing at Klosters with Prince Charles and his party. Lady Sarah, a former pupil at the same finishing school, had enjoyed herself there, but Lady Diana, though she improved her French, her skiing and her domestic science, was unhappy and left after a short while.

At that time, her father was seriously ill after a massive brain haemorrhage, and his wife Raine nursed him devotedly. As there was little Lady Diana could do to help, she went to live in a London flat owned by her father at Coleherne Court in South Kensington. One of her three companions was Carolyn Pride, her friend from West Heath School.

Althorp, the Northamptonshire family seat of the Spencer family.

27

Part of the magnificent collection of paintings at Althorp.

Lady Diana, like her sisters before her, had no wish to become a debutante, and once in London she took up a Cordon Bleu cookery course and busied herself looking after children. She had particular care of a two-year-old American boy, Patrick, playing games with him and taking him out for airings in his push-chair.

Her sister Lady Jane, who had been bridesmaid to Miss Katharine Worsley when she married the Duke of Kent in 1961, the year of Lady Diana's birth, was married in 1978 to Robert Fellowes, Assistant Private Secretary to the Queen since 1977, and son of Sir William Fellowes, for many years the Land Agent at Sandringham. Lady Diana was bridesmaid. Their eldest sister Lady Sarah, a goddaughter of the Queen Mother, is married to Captain Neil McCorquodale, ex-Coldstream Guards, and they farm in Lincolnshire.

Overleaf: The Rubens Room, Althorp.

Earl Spencer in the wine cellar at Althorp.

The tall, strikingly attractive Lady Diana was having a happy and carefree existence in London with friends of her own age and was often to be seen shopping locally or at the exclusive Knightsbridge stores. Soon after her seventeenth birthday she passed her driving test – first time. In 1979 she had her first car and later the famous red Metro in which she tried to elude the ever-present press corps who dogged her footsteps.

Holidays were spent at Althorp or with her mother in Scotland, and she enjoyed skiing in Switzerland. There were parties and dances, but in the spring of 1979 she decided to take a job. And it was one after her own heart. In the autumn term, Lady Diana began working at the Young England Kindergarten in Pimlico, run by her friends Mrs Victoria Wilson and Kay Seth-Smith who had both been at West Heath. She quickly endeared herself to her pupils, teaching them painting, dancing and

Right: Lady Jane Spencer, god-daughter of the Duke of Kent, posing outside the Guards Chapel, Wellington Barracks, London, after her marriage in April 1978 to Robert Fellowes. Lady Diana was a bridesmaid.

Above: The Earl and Countess Spencer attending a function at Corby Civic Hall.

drawing, and joining in the games which they all devised. She had had no formal training but was an instinctive 'natural' with the children, a characteristic she has shown all her life.

It was an exciting time for Lady Diana who was happy in her work and her flat, and enjoying the delights of living in London, where she could experiment with new and 'different' clothes. Her choice, which was to set a fashion trend nationwide, included culottes in corduroy, lambswool sweaters, cotton skirts and shirts from Laura Ashley, dresses and suits from Harrods, and clothes from Emanuel. Her jewellery was simple.

August 1979 brought a change. She was invited to Balmoral to join the royal houseparty as a guest of the Queen. She was just eighteen, and she and Prince Andrew who was nineteen enjoyed each other's company in the Scottish highlands. In February 1980 she was invited to Sandringham and revived memories of her happy childhood in Norfolk.

Inexorably, the wheels of her romance were set in motion. In July Prince Charles invited her to watch him playing for Les Diables Bleus at a polo match in Sussex. And a week or two later, she was the guest of the Royal Family on board the royal yacht *Britannia* during Cowes Week in August.

That was a busy month, for she travelled to Balmoral once more in the first week of September and was photographed fishing the River Dee with Prince Charles. Her name appeared in newspapers the world over, and for the next five months she was 'fair game' to newspaper reporters who dogged her movements relentlessly. Never once during this ordeal did her calm break: she did not falter or show anything other than the patience, consideration and amusement she would show one of her charges. Her impeccable behaviour won the respect and admiration of those who harassed her and the complete approval of the Royal Family, and the Prince of Wales in particular.

Speculation rose to new heights when in the autumn Prince Charles bought Highgrove House, a Georgian mansion a mile from Tetbury in Gloucestershire. It had been owned by Maurice Macmillan MP, son of the

Lady Diana's London flat on the first floor at Coleherne Court, South Kensington.

Carolyn Pride, Virginia Pitman and Ann Bolton, former flatmates of Lady Diana.

Right: Shopping at Harrods.

Above: Lady Sarah Spencer after her marriage to Neil McCorquodale.

former Prime Minister Harold Macmillan, and was a short distance from Gatcombe Park, the home of Princess Anne and Captain Mark Phillips.

There was complete privacy, which was exactly what the Prince required, and good access to London or the polo grounds at Cirencester, and there was excellent hunting, shooting and fishing in the locality.

At this time, the Prince and Lady Diana made many visits to the house, choosing decorations and planning their future home. The country house that would eventually be their first home had to be exactly right. The interior designer Dudley Poplek was asked to refurbish it according to their wishes, and piece by piece Highgrove was transformed.

In the dying months of 1980, every move of the Prince and Lady Diana was watched, and often he had to endure some good-natured teasing which he accepted with his usual humour. The couple had to resort to the technique of using several of the Prince's titles in communicating with each other: Charles Renfrew, Lord of the Isles, was one.

In November, the Prince gave a royal launch to BL's new Metro, taking it on a twenty-minute test drive at their plant at Longbridge. He must have liked the car, for soon afterwards Lady Diana was to be seen driving a red Metro in London, said to have been a present from the

Left: A classroom scene at the Young England Kindergarten, Pimlico, where Lady Diana worked.

Below: Lady Diana's arms full at the kindergarten!

Prince. All too soon this car was probably the best-known in London, as it was watched night and day by the media. When, on one occasion, Lady Diana ran the gauntlet of their persistent questioning and gained the comparative sanctuary of her car, she was justifiably annoyed when it stalled!

That same month Prince Charles rode his 'chaser Allibar in the Club Amateurs Riding Handicap Steeplechase at Ludlow and came second. An expert horseman, the Prince is known for his skill on the polo field and is now keenly pursuing his love of steeplechasing whenever he has a chance. The late Duke of Windsor, also a keen horseman when Prince of Wales, was persuaded to give up his steeplechasing efforts after a series of falls.

Princess Margaret celebrated her fiftieth birthday with a party at the Ritz Hotel in London in November which was attended by many members of the Royal Family. Lady Diana was also among the guests.

There was renewed speculation about wedding plans when Prince Charles celebrated his thirty-second birthday on 14 November. He had often said that thirty was a good age to marry, so press coverage of his birthdays after he passed that age was particularly keen. But there was no announcement, and he celebrated with a private dinner party.

His tour of India with its crowded schedule went ahead, and he was photographed sitting at the romantic Taj Mahal and in the bustling city of Calcutta, where he was obviously moved by his meeting with Mother

Above: Lady Diana at the Lambourn stables of Nick Gaselee.

Opposite page: With a wry smile, Lady Diana gets into her Metro, always pursued by photographers.

Above: The famous Metro discovered in a hiding place with its well-known owner!

Opposite page: Leaving the Ritz Hotel, London, after attending Princess Margaret's fiftieth birthday party.

Teresa and some of the people she tries to help. He returned home just before Christmas which came and went with no news of an engagement.

At Sandringham in January the Royal Family were literally besieged by the press, much to their annoyance. It must have seemed as if photographers and reporters were actually growing on the very trees in the grounds.

The wires buzzed with rumours and conjecture – every meeting, smile, frown was commented on. An early morning meeting between the Prince and Lady Diana at the home of Nick Gaselee, his racing trainer at Lambourn, was met with delight. Every 'sighting' at Highgrove or when they were reputedly seen in friends' houses was manna to the hungry presses.

Then there was a bonus. Buckingham Palace confirmed that Lady Diana had joined the Royal Family for a three-day stay at Sandringham, so legions of journalists flocked there.

Prince Charles, with the Duke and Duchess of Gloucester, paid his customary visit to Klosters in January for the skiing. This must have been hard for Lady Diana who also enjoys the sport.

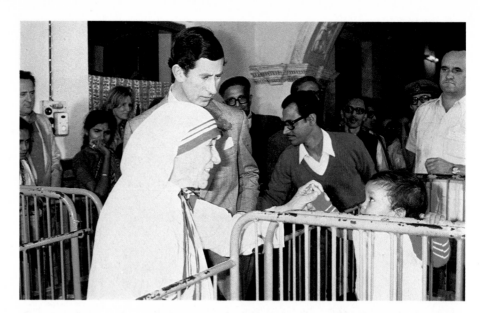

Right: Prince Charles is introduced to a patient by Mother Teresa at her mission in Calcutta.

Above: Enjoying a solitary walk at Althorp.

The third week of February saw a great sadness for Prince Charles. He visited his racing trainer's stables for a practice gallop on his 'chaser Allibar. Soon after he had mounted the horse faltered, and he dismounted quickly. Allibar died from a heart attack, his owner cradling his head in his arms. Lady Diana, who was watching, left with tears on her face, unable to offer comfort with so many spectators. The couple had to leave separately, though it was a mere three days before the announcement of their engagement.

At a private dinner in his sitting room at Buckingham Palace, Prince Charles proposed to Lady Diana Spencer, and she accepted. Soon afterwards she went to Australia for a short holiday with her mother, perhaps to escape the glare of publicity that awaited her. Unfortunately, they were the focus of world attention and were again harassed by constant pressure from the media.

In London Prince Charles told the Queen and the Duke of Edinburgh of his plans and, in an unusual gesture for these days, formally asked the Earl Spencer for his youngest daughter's hand in marriage. Permission was given.

The Engagement

It was on Tuesday, 24 February 1981, that at long, long last Buckingham Palace released the news the world had been waiting for. Prince Charles and Lady Diana Spencer were officially engaged.

Lord Maclean, the Lord Chamberlain, made the announcement to hundreds attending a routine Investiture, with the Queen smiling happily as he did so. Outside the band of the Coldstream Guards played the popular song 'Congratulations', and gradually the meaning of its insistent rhythm penetrated the minds of those listening. From one to another the message was passed, and there was great cheering.

The cold dull February day was enlivened by this spark, soon to be fanned into a flame, of joy which greeted the announcement. Economic gloom and winter were put aside in a general air of genuine pleasure and good wishes emphasizing the admiration and affection with which the Royal Family are regarded. There were good wishes from all over the world, but the enthusiasm was especially strong in the United Kingdom that the future King had chosen an English girl to be his bride. Her gentle simplicity was an instant attraction to all.

Outside Buckingham Palace, the hub of the capital, crowds gathered, and the news media were there in strength. The news was flashed on to BBC television screens, and later the lucky interviewer (who was getting

Crowds outside Buckingham Palace the day the royal engagement was announced.

41

Right: Earl and Countess Spencer in their London flat on the day of the engagement.

Above: A smiling Lady Fermoy, Lady Diana's grandmother.

Opposite page: The engagement day picture of Prince Charles and Lady Diana that was soon known worldwide.

crowd reaction) discovered the bride's father on the pavement. He had his camera and was taking photographs of the occasion. He said he was delighted and very proud and wanted to record the event – as he had done the earlier events of his daughters' lives.

Inside, to the accompaniment of chants of 'We want the Prince and Lady Diana', the bridal couple were having an informal lunch with the Queen and Prince Andrew who was on leave from the Royal Navy. Punctually, at 3 o'clock in the afternoon, they posed for the waiting photographers in the grounds of the Palace.

Wearing a blue silk suit, soon to be copied on book jackets, tea towels, postcards and a host of commemoratives, designed by Cojana, recent winners of the Queen's Award for Industry, Lady Diana smiled broadly. She happily showed her engagement ring – an oval sapphire surrounded by fourteen diamonds and set in eighteen-carat gold – twisting her hand one way and another for everyone to get the best pictures. It was immediately obvious to everyone that she was brimming with real happiness and wanted the whole world to share her joy.

Lady Diana was aware that, from 11 o'clock that morning, her life had changed and would never be the same again. The daily routine of sharing

a flat with three friends, shopping and going to work was no more, and she was immediately brought under the Buckingham Palace umbrella of protective protocol. She would live in royal palaces with servants to wait on her, and the watching world would be deprived of the sight of her driving the red Metro to and fro: now there would be a chauffeur and a detective on hand.

With instinctive kindness the Queen Mother invited her grandson's fiancée to stay with her at Clarence House after the announcement. There Lady Diana would have all the help and encouragement she needed and could call on her personal knowledge, as one who had trodden a similar path herself. Her grandmother, Lady Fermoy, was of course also at Clarence House to give advice and guidance in the weeks ahead.

The wheels of national participation were beginning to grind all over the country. The Archbishop of Canterbury, Dr Robert Runcie, interrupted a debate (appropriately enough on the subject of marriage) of the General Synod of the Church of England to announce the engagement, and the Prime Minister, Margaret Thatcher, informed the House of Commons. The Members of Parliament showed their delight at the news by sending the couple a congratulatory message.

Waving through the rain, Lady Diana leaves for Clarence House on her engagement day.

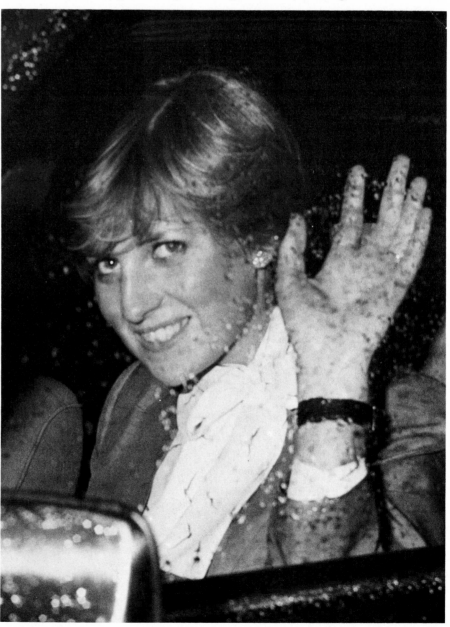

44

Leaving her London flat with her personal detective after her engagement had been announced.

The people of the tiny Gloucestershire village of Doughton, a mile from Prince Charles's home at Highgrove, had their own celebration. They marked the occasion by placing a red carpet in the one and only public telephone box.

At long last, Prince Charles had found a girl to share his life, and his fiancée was surely everything he could have wished for. Growing up almost in their shadow made her at ease with his family, and she shared his love for music and the arts, as well as the outdoor life.

Tall and graceful, with silver blonde hair cut in a deceptively casual style, she was happiest in simple clothes with the minimum of jewellery. Her steady blue eyes held a hint of mischief, and she laughed easily. Inevitably, she would lead the young fashions, though she was not trendy, and already her clothes and hairstyle have been copied by many girls all over the world.

The nation was delighted with her and perhaps relieved that the Prince had chosen an English girl obviously possessed of dignity and a quiet strength as his future bride. The fact that she was beautiful was an added bonus. The girl, who somehow had always been waiting in the wings, had found the love of her Prince Charming, the Prince of Wales. The nineteen-year-old girl was to marry a man twelve years her senior, but there was a good balance in the extrovert Prince and his lovely shy bride with a mind of her own.

It was inevitable that the Prince and Lady Diana should have to appear on the television after the photographers had clicked their camera shutters red-hot with pictures. So, relaxed and happy, the newly engaged couple answered the searching questions, and Lady Diana admitted to feeling nervous while the Prince said he preferred summer to winter weddings. Naturally, after months of press frustration at the lack of real news, the interviewers wanted every single detail. Asked where they had met, the Prince replied it was in 1977 in a field, and added that he had thought the sixteen-year-old was 'jolly, amusing and attractive, bouncy and full of life and everything'. They both agreed they loved music and outdoor pursuits such as skiing and walking, and then went on to speak of their love for each other and the problems besetting a royal romance. Lady Diana affirmed that 'with Prince Charles next to me I can't go wrong', and they both were 'delighted and happy' and 'of course in love'.

45

Right: An evening at the Royal Opera House when Prince Charles and Lady Diana saw a performance of L'Africaine.

Below: On 1 March the Prince and Lady Diana attended a service at a private chapel on the Cheshire estate of the Marquess of Cholmondeley.

Opposite page: In a striking dress that set a new fashion, Lady Diana accompanied the Prince on their first public engagement, a Gala Evening at the Goldsmiths' Hall in London.

So far, no actual date had been fixed for the Royal Wedding, though the end of the summer was hinted at, and many speculated the service would follow royal tradition and take place in Westminster Abbey.

To the chants of the hopeful swelling crowds that called for a balcony appearance, Lady Diana was driven away, a policeman at her side, to start her new life. Later that evening she and her fiancé dined at Clarence House with their respective grandmothers and emerged to wave to the crowds who had gathered in the Mall in the hope of catching a glimpse of them and wishing them well on this happy day.

So began the busy round of royal duties in a month crowded with engagements, and the bride-to-be quickly learned in the days that followed how much the ever-eager public demand of their royals.

March was a month of firsts – a new beginning to a different life and engagements ranging from their shared interest in music to state banquets, with two race meetings and 'walkabouts' in the comparative peace of Gloucestershire in between. It was the same everywhere: everyone wanted to see Lady Diana, and her every move was watched with a new interest.

Lady Diana's name appeared regularly in the Court Circulars, and rooms were set aside for her at Buckingham Palace for dressmaker fittings, discussions as to the arrangements and preparations. Oliver Everett, a former diplomat and assistant private secretary to Prince Charles, became her unofficial private secretary to cope with the flood of telegrams and letters of congratulation that poured in from all over the world.

While staying with their friends Lord and Lady Cholmondeley at Cholmondeley Castle in Cheshire, the Prince of Wales and his fiancée celebrated St David's Day on 1 March by attending service in the private chapel. Another private occasion was an evening at the Royal Opera

House, Covent Garden, where they went to hear Meyerbeer's opera *L'Africaine*.

The pieces of the Royal Wedding jigsaw were beginning to take shape. First, it was announced that the wedding would take place on 29 July, and that the day would be a public holiday. Then came the, to some, surprise news that the service would be in St Paul's Cathedral, a break with the royal tradition of marriages taking place in Westminster Abbey. The last royal bride to marry there, in 1973, was Princess Anne, who was expecting her second child in May.

Prince Charles and Lady Diana's first official public engagement was to attend a recital at Goldsmiths' Hall in London in aid of the Royal Opera House Development Appeal. Dense crowds gathered outside to welcome them, and Lady Diana was met with delighted cheers of warm approval. She wore a striking black taffeta off-the-shoulder dress designed for the occasion by David and Elizabeth Emanuel, which, with glittering diamonds, set off her figure to full advantage, enhancing her fair colouring.

This special evening of music, poetry and prose was a memorable occasion in which Her Serene Highness Princess Grace of Monaco took part with other stars. Lady Diana was presented with a single pink rose which soon became the buttonhole of Prince Charles, a gesture which endeared her to many. It was the first of the many floral gifts she would receive.

At the reception afterwards attended by 285 guests, the serenely happy Lady Diana was able to meet many of the Prince's friends at the Royal Opera House, and over £7000 was raised for the Appeal.

The loyal crowds who waited in the cold night air for another glimpse of the lovely Lady Diana were not disappointed, and they cheered as, smiling and waving happily, the couple left.

Below: Prince Charles and Lady Diana with Princess Grace of Monaco who recited her poems at the Goldsmiths' Hall on 9 March.

Next day it was announced that David and Elizabeth Emanuel, who had created the sensational black ballgown for Lady Diana to wear at the Goldsmiths' Hall, would design and make the wedding dress, another indication that the bride wished to establish her own style and fashion sense.

Friday the 13th was an unlucky day for Prince Charles. Watched by his grandmother the Queen Mother, his aunt Princess Margaret and his fiancée, he rode his horse Good Prospect in the Grand Military Cup at Sandown. Unfortunately, he was 'dislodged' at the eighteenth fence, though his only injury was a bloody nose. Five days later at the National Hunt Festival Meeting at Cheltenham, the Prince and Good Prospect parted company at the tenth fence in the Kim Muir Memorial Challenge Cup. Lady Diana was again a spectator, and that evening she attended her first State Banquet at Buckingham Palace. With Prince Charles she was among those who welcomed President Shagari of Nigeria who was in England on a State Visit.

As the month drew to a close, engagements followed in quick succession. In a helicopter piloted by Prince Charles, he and Lady Diana paid an official visit to Cheltenham, this time to the headquarters of the Gloucestershire police, the force responsible for their safety while in residence at Highgrove House at Tetbury. They toured the buildings and even had a word for the police horses in their stables. A schoolboy in the cheering crowd presented Lady Diana with a daffodil and asked if he might kiss her hand. Blushing slightly but laughing, she agreed, and he had a moment to remember all his life.

Top: Prince Charles talking to his aunt in the paddock before racing at Sandown.

Above: An anxious Lady Diana watches as Prince Charles falls from his horse at Sandown Races.

Right and below right: An informal walkabout at Tetbury, near Highgrove.

Above: A gallant schoolboy kisses Lady Diana's hand at Cheltenham.

In their 'home' county, they took time for a long walkabout in Tetbury where the local residents turned out in force to welcome them. The small town was gay with bunting and flags, and there was a festival atmosphere as they walked among the crowds, shaking hands and exchanging a word with as many people as possible. The familiar pattern of royal walkabouts was taking shape, and soon Lady Diana's arms were filled with flowers, some single blooms, others posies and formal bunches pressed into her hands. With unflagging zeal, Lady Diana moved among the crowds, making the acquaintance of her new neighbours who were more than eager to welcome her, and the readiness with which she bent down to speak to children won her many hearts. Prince Charles was to open a new operating theatre at the local hospital, and Lady Diana took some of her flowers with her, offering them to the patients with the suggestion that they 'might like to share these flowers', tactfully avoiding any disappointment to anyone who had given them. The disabled people lining the route to the hospital were not forgotten, and the couple stopped for a special word with them and a share in the flowers.

A large piece of the background to the jigsaw was now fitted into place. The Queen held a meeting of the Privy Council at Buckingham Palace so that it could give its formal consent to the marriage. Such consent is required under the Royal Marriages Act of 1772, or to give it its full title 'an Act for better regulating the future marriages of the Royal Family'. Afterwards the Queen posed with the Prince and Lady Diana for the official photographs, then for the first time photographs were taken of the Privy Council with the Sovereign and Prince Charles.

All too soon the inevitability of the royal discipline was to pierce the bubble of Lady Diana's happiness. On 29 March, two days after the meeting of the Privy Council, the Prince of Wales had to leave for a long-arranged five-week tour of New Zealand, Australia, Venezuela and America. At Heathrow Airport he kissed Lady Diana, bravely smiling with tear-filled eyes, and she watched his plane taxi across the tarmac and take off. From now on until his return in May, her only contact with him would be by telephone and messages and by watching him on newsreels.

Coinciding with the Prince's arrival in New Zealand, Buckingham

Palace gave more details of the wedding arrangements, and his fiancée was busily visiting dressmakers and milliners, choosing her trousseau and attending to the hundred and one details that face any bride. Already she was practising walking with a train, by using, as have so many before her, a sheet pinned to her shoulders.

The Archbishop of Canterbury, Dr Robert Runcie, was to conduct the marriage service in St Paul's. It would be his first Royal Wedding service, and the Speaker of the House of Commons, the Right Hon. George Thomas, would read the Lesson. Prayers would be offered by a former Archbishop of Canterbury, Lord Coggan, and by the Cardinal Archbishop of Westminster and the Moderator of the General Assembly of the Church of Scotland. Thus there would be a blend of all the denominations of the Church for this happy occasion.

The Queen and Prince Charles with members of the Privy Council after the formal approval of the royal marriage. This is the first-ever photograph of the Council with the Queen and the Prince of Wales.

Right: Prince Charles getting down to his audience in New Zealand.

Below: The first parting. Lady Diana says farewell to Prince Charles at Heathrow airport as he sets off on a five-week tour.

Right: The Royal Navy in New Zealand as a joke presented the Prince with a ball and chain as a Wedding present.

There would be five attendants for Lady Diana, led by the eldest, Lady Sarah Armstrong-Jones, daughter of Princess Margaret and a cousin of Prince Charles. She had been a bridesmaid to Lady Sarah Spencer, sister of the bride, at her marriage to Captain Neil McCorquodale at Althorp in 1980, the first Spencer family wedding there since 1914 when Lady Delia Peel was married.

The other bridesmaids were India Hicks, daughter of David and Lady Pamela Hicks and grand-daughter of Lord Mountbatten; Sarah Jane Gaselee, the eleven-year-old daughter of Nick Gaselee who trains Prince Charles's racehorse; Catherine Cameron, the seven-year-old daughter of Donald Cameron of Lochiel and Lady Cecil Cameron; and the youngest child, Clementine Hambro, five-year-old great grand-daughter of Sir Winston Churchill and a pupil at the Young England Kindergarten in Pimlico where Lady Diana had worked.

Lord Nicholas Windsor, eleven-year-old son of the Duke and Duchess of Kent, and Edward van Cutsem, nine-year-old son of Mr and Mrs Hugh van Cutsem, would be pages.

In accordance with royal tradition, the Prince would not have a best man. Instead, he would be attended by two supporters, his brothers Prince Andrew and Prince Edward.

A little light relief came for Lady Diana when with her friends the Hon. Nicholas Soames and his fiancée Catherine Weatherall she was one of a party at the Shaftesbury Theatre to see *They're Playing Our Song*, and next day she visited the Queen at Windsor on the occasion of Her Majesty's fifty-fifth birthday.

Prince Charles was now in Australia where he apologized for his fiancée's absence, but promised they would return together later, to the delight of his audiences.

A visit to Venezuela and then to the United States of America to see President Reagan in Washington completed the royal tour.

The Prince returned to Britain in an RAF VC10 on Sunday, 3 May, landing at RAF Lossiemouth in Scotland. At once he drove to Balmoral where a delighted Lady Diana was waiting for him. Her British Airways

Top: One of the royal bridesmaids, Sarah Jane Gaselee, daughter of Prince Charles's trainer Nick Gaselee.

Above: The van Cutsem boys. Edward, on the left, was one of the pages at the Wedding.

Left: Prince Charles in conversation with President Reagan at the White House in Washington, D.C.

53

flight from Heathrow to Aberdeen had been beset by thunderstorms, and the plane was struck by lightning; but she landed safely to welcome her fiancé home to a short holiday.

For a few days the Prince and Lady Diana had a peaceful holiday at Balmoral, and she learned to fish on the River Dee under the watchful eye of the Prince and estate ghillies. They were able to catch up on all the wedding news and preparations, not least the many, many presents that arrived by every post. Of course, the press and media were never far away, and Prince Charles and Lady Diana charmingly posed for photographs, the Prince's labrador Harvey with them. On their return to London, he caused some amusement by refusing to leave the plane on landing and had to be called sternly to order by his royal master!

At the Royal Naval Air Station at Culdrose in Cornwall, Prince Andrew, one of the supporters at the wedding, had received his wings from his father the Duke of Edinburgh after successfully completing his helicopter course.

Prince Charles and Lady Diana undertook a pleasant nostalgic duty in

Prince Charles and Lady Diana with Harvey at Balmoral.

Left: Lady Diana learning the skill of fly-fishing from Charlie Wright, head gamekeeper at Balmoral.

early May when they visited Broadlands, the Hampshire home of the late Lord Mountbatten, to open the Mountbatten Exhibition in his great-uncle's honour. Lady Diana wore an attractive green outfit, with one of her now familiar 'choirboy ruffles' blouses which, with her neat distinctive hairstyle, made a perfect foil for her impish radiant face. She seemed in her element, laughing and joking as they planted the commemorative trees.

For the Prince the visit must have been a nostalgic reminder of the many happy hours he had spent at Broadlands with Lord Mountbatten, and perhaps it was then that plans were set in motion for the royal honeymoon. For, like his mother and father before him, Prince Charles and his wife would spend the first nights of their honeymoon there, amid a host of memories and the beautiful peaceful Hampshire countryside that Lord Mountbatten loved so well.

Following a tradition started in 1937 with the Coronation of George VI, the Royal Jubilee Trusts, originally set up by King George V in 1935, published an Official Souvenir of the Royal Wedding, with photographs of the couple and their families and biographical notes, all fully illustrated in colour. Of course it was a sell-out, and the proceeds, in the International Year of Disabled People, went to help the handicapped. The Prince of Wales is Patron of the International Year of Disabled People in Britain.

The wedding ring was to be made of Welsh gold taken from the same nugget used for the wedding rings of Queen Elizabeth the Queen Mother in 1923, the Queen in 1947, Princess Margaret in 1960 and Princess Anne in 1973, thus preserving a long link. The original nugget had been found in a mine in Bontddu, Gwynedd, and the owner kept the remainder after the first ring had been made in 1923 for the then Lady

Above: Returning from Balmoral, Harvey refuses to leave the plane until Prince Charles calls him to heel.

55

*Opposite page, top: Collingwood,
the Queen's goldsmiths and
jewellers in Conduit Street,
London, who made the Princess's
wedding ring.*

*Right: Making friends on
walkabout at Broadlands.*

*Below: Watched by a smiling
Prince Charles, Lady Diana
treeplanting at Broadlands.*

Elizabeth Bowes-Lyon for her marriage to the Duke of York. The goldsmith W. J. L. Bertolle bought the gold, offering it to Princess Elizabeth for her wedding, and it is said that Lady Diana's ring is all that remains of the nugget. It is particularly appropriate that this last piece of Welsh gold be used to make the ring for the new Princess of Wales.

May continued its round of engagements, and the Prince and his fiancée were present at the lunch given by the Queen at Windsor in honour of the President of Ghana. In the afternoon Lady Diana watched as Her Majesty presented new Colours to the 1st Battalion the Welsh Guards, of which Prince Charles is Colonel-in-Chief. Afterwards they all attended a party at Victoria Barracks.

Princess Anne gave birth to a daughter, Zara, on 15 May and was visited by her brother and his fiancée while in hospital. They also attended a dedication service at Tetbury parish church near their home at Highgrove and received a warm welcome from their growing number of friends there.

Prince Charles was best man to the Hon. Nicholas Soames when he married Catherine Weatherall at St Margaret's, Westminster, and Lady Diana, in a stunning red outfit with picture hat, was present with members of the Royal Family. Clementine Hambro, who was to be one of the bridesmaids on 29 July, was bridesmaid on this occasion, eagerly watched by her former teacher.

There were two State Banquets to follow during the State Visit of King Khaled of Saudi Arabia, one given by the Queen at Buckingham Palace

Above: Lady Diana at Windsor Castle to watch the Queen present new Colours to the First Battalion of the Welsh Regiment of Foot Guards of which the Prince of Wales is Colonel.

and another by the King at Claridge's. Both were attended by the Prince and his fiancée.

The couple went to St Paul's Cathedral to hear the music chosen for their wedding, and another rehearsal of the service. They lunched with the Archbishop of Canterbury and discussed the arrangements. Later, it was announced that Lady Diana would swear to 'love, honour and cherish', not to 'obey', her husband.

The Queen's Official Birthday Parade, or Trooping the Colour, on Horse Guards Parade took place with its customary military precision, and Lady Diana, wearing a very feminine pale blue outfit topped by a small hat, watched with other members of the Royal Family as the Queen took the salute. Her Majesty was unperturbed by a dramatic incident which had taken place earlier when blank shots were fired near her. The traditional balcony appearance for the fly-past afterwards was another new experience for the Prince's fiancée.

As a lady of a Knight Companion of the Order, Lady Diana attended the Order of the Garter Service of Thanksgiving at St George's Chapel, Windsor. And so Royal Ascot Week began in the time-honoured manner.

Below: With Prince Andrew as escort, Lady Diana attends the Trooping the Colour ceremony on Horse Guards Parade.

Right: Members of the Royal Family with Lady Diana at the wedding of Nicholas Soames in London.

Above: On the balcony of
Buckingham Palace with the Royal
Family after watching the
Trooping the Colour ceremony in
June.

Right: As a lady of a Knight
Companion of the Order of the
Garter, Lady Diana attended the
annual service at Windsor.

Overleaf: In a stunning outfit of grey and white, Lady Diana is escorted by Prince Charles on the last day of Royal Ascot.

Left: On the first day of Royal Ascot Lady Diana wore a striking lilac and white striped outfit with a lilac hat trimmed with ostrich feathers.

Below: Lady Diana is the centre of attraction on the third day of Royal Ascot.

*Above: Lady Diana strolling in
the Royal Enclosure on the last day
of the races.*

The crowd of racegoers who lined the course to cheer the royal party as
their carriages drove down the course were not disappointed. All eyes
were on the Prince of Wales and Lady Diana. Her clothes were a delight.
The first day, sitting beside the Prince, her lilac and white striped dress was
topped by a feminine picture hat of the same lilac shade edged with
feathers in a frond. The second day of the royal meeting, while the Prince
flew in Concorde to New York to attend a gala performance by the Royal
Ballet, his fiancée's appearance at the races was another outstanding
success. In bright red and with a jaunty straw boater, she looked charming
as she walked about the Royal Enclosure and Paddock. All eyes were on
her again the next day: with Princess Alexandra at her side, she was
elegant in pale cream and an attractive hat with a single flower. After a
gruelling trip, Prince Charles returned to be at Royal Ascot for the last day
of the meeting.

The Week ended with a belated twenty-first birthday celebration ball
at Windsor for Prince Andrew, whose actual birthday had been in
February, just before the engagement was announced. Some six hundred
guests danced until the early hours – and it was Lady Diana's dress they all
remembered.

Two more glittering occasions followed – a soirée at the Royal
Academy of Arts and a Gala Première at the Odeon, Leicester Square, of
the James Bond film *For Your Eyes Only*. A crowded week ended with a
visit to the Military Musical Pageant at Wembley Stadium with the
Prince and Lady Diana gracing the events.

*Opposite page: Lady Diana fulfils
an evening engagement at the
Royal Academy.*

The day before his future wife's twentieth birthday Prince Charles gave a garden party at Highgrove for hundreds of tenants from the Duchy of Cornwall, and they were all delighted to meet a relaxed and happy Lady Diana who was still smiling in spite of all the pressures of the previous few weeks.

And so to July and the Wedding drawing ever nearer. Lady Diana's birthday on 1 July was quietly celebrated with her fiancé, family and friends.

Lady Diana paid three visits to Wimbledon, two with her sisters, to see the Men's Singles semi-finals and later the finals won by John McEnroe. And she was there, smiling and clapping, when Chris Evert Lloyd won the Women's Singles title again.

The first official portrait of Lady Diana by Bryan Organ was hung at the National Portrait Gallery where it was the immediate focus of attention. The artist, who had already painted Prince Charles, portrayed her in a relaxed casual style sitting sideways in a chair against a plain background at Buckingham Palace. Unfortunately, the painting was later vandalized, but after repair by the Gallery it again hangs next to that of Prince Charles, by the same artist, in the National Portrait Gallery.

BBC Television screened a documentary on the life of the Prince of Wales, *A Prince for Our Time*, which gave a fascinating background to the Heir to the Throne.

In the last week before the Wedding, as guests were arriving, the bride and groom continued their hectic programme. The Prince played polo in the British Open Championships at Windsor and Cowdray Park. Lady Diana had a final fitting of her wedding dress and attended another rehearsal in St Paul's in the evening. There was a small stag party for the Prince.

Above: Lady Diana applauding a Wimbledon winner with Prince Albert and Princess Stephanie of Monaco.

Opposite page: Looking dazzling, Lady Diana attends the première of the James Bond film For Your Eyes Only *at the Odeon, Leicester Square in London. The film was shown in aid of the NSPCC.*

Above: Bryan Organ's portrait of the Princess of Wales at the National Portrait Gallery, London.

Right: Prince Charles and Lady Diana relaxing at a polo match.

Opposite page: Informal attire for the bride-to-be at a polo match at Cowdray Park.

Right: An informal picture of Prince Charles and Lady Diana at a polo match just before the Wedding.

Below: Prince Andrew and Prince Charles join Lady Diana to watch polo.

Left: Lady Diana with members of the Royal Family at a garden party at Buckingham Palace in July.

On 23 July Prince Charles and Lady Diana were interviewed at Buckingham Palace for the BBC and ITV by Angela Rippon and Andrew Gardner. A relaxed and happy bride-to-be spoke of her feelings of gratitude to all those who had sent presents and good wishes. She said she had been especially touched by the many children who had made things for them including lots of cakes decorated with Smarties. Televised the day before the wedding, the interview made a lovely prologue.

The Prince played another polo match at Windsor for England II against Spain, and his team were victorious. The Queen gave a private party for close friends and guests at Buckingham Palace, and all was in readiness for the great event.

The wedding festivities literally started with a bang! A huge firework display with a specially constructed palace façade was set up in Hyde Park in London, and a crowd of more than half a million gathered in the warm sunshine to watch. They started arriving early in the day to take up positions and waited and waited in happy good humour.

71

Opposite page, top: Lady Diana talking to ten-year-old Dean Brown as Prince Charles takes the salute at HMS Mercury near Petersfield.

Right: The Prince and Lady Diana during their television interview shown the evening before the Wedding.

In the evening the Queen and other members of the Royal Family with their distinguished guests arrived to watch from specially constructed stands. Everyone cheered enthusiastically at the unusual sight of Kings and Queens, Presidents and their ladies and many other dignitaries arriving by coach to join in the fun.

At precisely 10.08 pm the Prince lit the first of a nationwide chain of 101 ·beacons and bonfires, and soon the night sky was ablaze, sending the message across the world. At Althorp, Lady Diana's brother Lord Charles Althorp drank the health of the bridal couple and put a torch to the flames, a scene repeated many times that night.

The firework display, the biggest of its kind in Britain for over two hundred years, was accompanied by the music of the Household Musicians, the singing of the Morrison Orpheus Choir and the Choir of the Welsh Guards. The King's Troop Royal Horse Artillery fired salvoes, and the amazing spectacular included the biggest Catherine wheel in the

Below: Lord Althorp drinking a toast to the bride and groom after lighting the Althorp bonfire.

Bottom and overleaf: The pre-Wedding firework display in Hyde Park.

world – some 40 ft (12 m) across – whose fire spread over a diameter of 100 ft (30 m).

The crackle, the splutter, the diamond-like stars in the sky, the flash of radiance rising to brilliant incandescence seemed to hover and hesitate as if reluctant to die away.

So in dazzling effervescent style, the celebrations for the Royal Wedding began, and the brightness and joy set the pattern for the happiness of the morning to come.

Wedding Fever

As soon as the Royal Engagement was announced in February, the Buckingham Palace machinery, so used to coping admirably with every occasion however special, swung into top gear. The coveted invitations were sent out, the Lord Chamberlain, Lord Maclean, took over the arrangements and the careful detailed planning began. He had last planned such an event when Princess Anne had married Captain Mark Phillips in November 1973.

There was a great deal to do. The Lord Chamberlain's office was responsible for many things including the accommodation and hospitality necessary for the countless overseas guests who would be in London, as well as the overall responsibility for the arrangements within the Palace itself. Here there would be the catering, the staff needed on the domestic and the secretarial side, and the many, many details so often taken for granted. Everything had to be perfect, as always.

Lord Maclean also had to plan the processional route for the journey to St Paul's from the Palace, which was longer than that to Westminster Abbey used in the past, and this meant even more precise attention to detail for the carriage processions with their escorts to and from the Cathedral. Thousands of troops would line the route, and the Queen's personal bodyguards of the Yeomen of the Guard and the Honourable Corps of Gentlemen-at-Arms would be on duty in the Cathedral, with the added anxiety of security in these days of terrorism.

The Archbishop of Canterbury and the Dean of St Paul's, with their advisers, planned the service, and the musicians began rehearsing the music chosen by the Prince and his fiancée. The Cathedral staff set about their task of all the special cleaning, refurbishing and preparation that would be needed. There was the added complication of the television cameras for the event which attracted world-wide interest. They had to be placed so as not to interfere with the service itself, yet to give maximum vision to the viewers. Everything had to be carefully timed to the last second to cater for the estimated audience of some 750 million all over the world. Never before had any event aroused such a response. Every step of the route had to be covered, and the world was anxious not to miss a single blink!

The security forces would be there in great strength with helicopters, tracker dogs and police marksmen on rooftops, for nothing could be left to chance.

From the outset, it was evident that Prince Charles and Lady Diana wanted their wedding celebrations to reflect the dedicated caring attitude

An anxious moment for Lord Maclean, the Lord Chamberlain, during the Wedding preparations.

Left: The chief organizers behind the scenes to ensure everything goes perfectly on the day. They are responsible for transport, police, royal gardens, etc.

Below left: The Dean of St Paul's.

Below: Nipper the ferret was used to pull cable through pipes for the TV pictures.

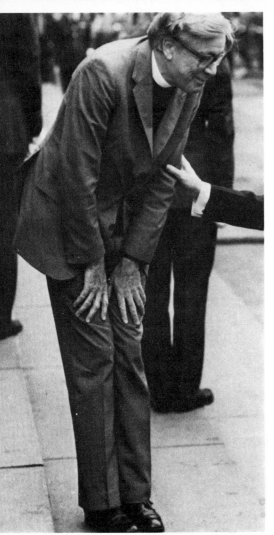

Right: Police marksmen take up positions.

An engineer placing a microwave dish to carry the television pictures on the day.

always shown by the Prince to which his future bride so readily subscribed. The service itself was a departure from other Royal Weddings by its ecumenical style and the inclusion of prayers from the Cardinal Archbishop of Westminster, the first time this had happened since the Reformation.

The specially chosen music would include an aria sung by the Maori opera singer Kiri Te Kanawa of New Zealand. The acoustics of the Cathedral would be given full rein with the musical programme planned by the Prince. No less than three choirs, members of three orchestras, four conductors and two groups of trumpeters to sound the triumphant fanfares would be there. The great organ would thunder out to blend with the crescendo of sound that would roll and echo around the magnificent building. A new version of the National Anthem, including side drums, was to be played, with a floating descant from the trumpeters. The music was British throughout, with a specially commissioned setting of Psalm 67 by the Welsh composer William Matthias, and a set of sung Versicles and Responses by Christopher Dearnley, the organist of St Paul's. Trumpeters would sound an echoing fanfare from the Whispering Gallery, and the music of Handel, who once played the organ at the Cathedral, would combine unforgettably with Sir Christopher Wren's soaring arches and domes.

Time was short for all the rehearsals needed to perfect the performances, and over and over again the sounds rang in the vast, usually empty Cathedral. Changes were made to allow for crowds and atmospheric conditions. The bellringers were to ring out 5000 changes of Stedman Cinques, making a four-hour pull for the thirteen ringers. They belong, as do all City ringers, to the Ancient Society of College Youths dating back to the seventeenth century. It would be their triumphant notes that would send the message 'They are married' all over the great City of London and the world.

Below left: A choirboy gets a Wedding haircut.

Below: A pre-Wedding rehearsal.

Bottom: The St Paul's choirboys.

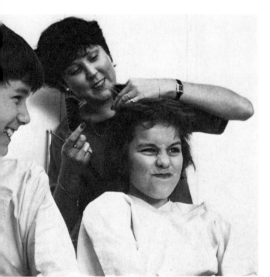

79

Stopwatch in hand, the Lord Chamberlain's Secretary times another rehearsal.

Right: A sergeant major gives the word!

Very early in those summer mornings, carriage processions would set out from the Royal Mews at Buckingham Palace along the processional routes, with careful precision. First one horse, then another would be chosen for colour and temperament, and even the infantry and other members of the armed services who would line the route played their pre-wedding roles. Many busloads of personnel were brought to the strategic points again and again, and the timing checked to ensure they would all be in place at the appointed time. Even the rotas of the Metropolitan and City of London police forces had to be checked and re-checked, and leave changed to ensure a full muster when it was particularly needed. Apart from the uniformed men, many plain-clothes officers would mingle with the crowds, and the police horses had a special part to play, for it was their duty to accompany Lady Diana from Clarence House to St Paul's on 29 July.

All over the country the threads of the wedding tapestry were coming together.

In Potterne, a tiny Wiltshire village, calligrapher Henry Fisher was working on the special marriage licence in his studio. For over thirty years he had performed the task of inscribing the Royal Wedding licences, his first being for the Queen and Prince Philip in 1947.

The present licence, measuring some 26 × 22 inches (660 × 560 mm), had to be engrossed with a turkey quill on parchment in red, blue and gold. It contained some 727 words and took about twelve hours to complete. Such a licence would cost hundreds of pounds commercially, but it was the wish of Henry Fisher and the parchment company that this one should be a gift to the Prince and Lady Diana.

A special licence has to be issued for any Royal Wedding for which the Queen has to give her consent; it will be kept in the Palace archives.

One of the most closely guarded of all the wedding secrets was that of the dress Lady Diana would wear. The designers, David and Elizabeth

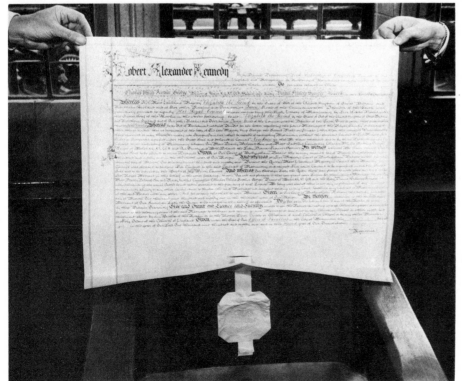

Above: David and Elizabeth Emanuel, who designed the Wedding dress, at their Mayfair workroom.

Left: The Royal Wedding licence.

Barbara Daly, the bride's make-up artist, practises her skills in preparation for the big day.

Emanuel, working from their Mayfair salon, had set up their couture house four years before. Young and imaginative, they met at art college when Welsh-born David came to the Harrow College of Art where Elizabeth was also a student. She was the daughter of a member of the WRNS and an American GI who settled in England after the war.

David is a talented musician, and Elizabeth, who studied with the Ballet Rambert, has excelled as a horsewoman, winning her class at the Royal International and Horse of the Year Shows at Wembley.

In 1977 the couple, who had married while at art school, set up their own couture business, and an almost fairy-tale picture emerges.

Bianca Jagger wore one of their dresses for the sensational horseback entry for her birthday party, and the Emanuels were famous. Their extravagantly skirted evening dresses soon established their reputation, and Lady Diana was first introduced to them through Lord Snowdon. He picked her as one of the beautiful women he wanted to photograph for *Vogue* magazine who chose her clothes. Lady Diana liked the pink chiffon blouse she wore and has bought other dresses.

The style of the wedding dress was a close secret, but the material was to be silk. It must shimmer under the television lights, must be full enough to allow the bride to move easily from her carriage to the altar, and, of paramount importance, must make her feel the happiest and most beautiful woman in the world.

The Lullingstone Silk Farm in Dorset made the silk for the Coronation robes of King George VI, and also the dress and the train for the Queen's wedding in 1947. The silkworms have to be fed on mulberry leaves which are grown with some difficulty, and some thousand metres of silk are reeled from each cocoon in a continuous filament, and then woven to produce a fabric.

The wedding bouquet and attendants' flowers had to be in keeping with royal tradition and also complement the bridal gown, so much care had to be taken to choose the right flowers, shape and overall effect.

Another innovation was the choice of the Senior Service, the Royal Navy, to make the wedding cake. Under the expert guidance of Chief Petty Officer David Avery RN, the cake was designed by the Naval Technical Drawing Department, and made at the Royal Naval Cookery School HMS *Pembroke* at Chatham. This was a great honour for the Navy and a fillip to the base at Chatham now threatened with closure.

Rising five tiers, it was made in March to give time for the flavour to improve, and four weeks were allowed for the icing. Tremendous care was taken, and every raisin was hand-picked. It took half an hour to crack all the eggs needed, one at a time, and though the recipe was secret, there can be little doubt traditional Navy rum was among the ingredients. The five tiers were decorated with pastel tinted plaques showing places connected with the couple, and it was safely delivered to the Palace in

The Royal Wedding cake made by the Royal Navy. Some of the proud chefs are beside it.

plenty of time. (Prince Charles cut the cake at the reception with his ceremonial sword.)

At the 1981 Chelsea Flower Show in London, the largest exhibit was the royal cypher made up of a circle of tiny green plants, 16 ft (nearly 5 m) in diameter. It was specially designed so that the twelve parts, each in a tray about 8 inches (20 cm) in depth, fitted closely together to form a circle with its joins invisible to the naked eye. Each tray was simple to move without harming the plants.

This was made in honour of the Royal Wedding by the gardeners in the Royal Parks and designed by the supervisor Bob Legge, whose special skill is landscaping, and the Royal Bailiff in charge of the Royal Parks, Ashley Stevenson, suggested that it be placed in Hyde Park for the summer. There it was a special delight to the visitors staying in Park Lane.

The royal gardeners planned the floral street decorations with the theme of pink, purple and silver, the same chosen for the Queen's Silver Jubilee celebrations in 1977. The pale colours were chosen because there would be a great deal of scarlet in the capital in the uniforms of the escorts and troops lining the routes, apart from the thousands of Union Jacks flying from buildings.

It was planned to have hanging baskets of flowers at the entrance of Clarence House as a foil for Lady Diana as she left for St Paul's with her father. Curiously enough, it would be the first time in its history that a bride had left Clarence House for her marriage.

Taffy the goat on parade with the Royal Regiment of Wales.

A detachment of the Life Guards on duty in London.

More baskets would adorn the lamp posts and flagpoles around the Victoria Memorial facing Buckingham Palace, these to be filled with verbena and petunias to give scent and colour.

About a million plants are grown annually from seed in the greenhouses of the Royal Parks, and some six thousand of these would be used for the Royal Wedding decorations.

The flagpoles along the route, forty-two in all, would carry a crown, the symbol of royalty, and the lamp posts have floral collars of baskets with the theme of the pink, purple and silver flowers repeated.

One of London's livery companies, the Worshipful Company of Gardeners, with the aid of the flower arrangers of the Cathedral, were to decorate its interior, with its special summer theme of simple daisy chains and Prince of Wales feathers in pampas grass garlanding the stone pillars, as well as the special set pieces.

One task that faced the royal gardeners was that of keeping the thousands of blooms fresh and sweet-smelling. Men could be seen carefully watering once the decorations were in place!

All would have a mounted escort from the Household Cavalry, and it is of interest to realize how long it takes the average trooper in the Sovereign's Escort to prepare for such an event. A trooper has to clean every item of his kit every day. He does the wet cleaning first, blancoing the buckskin breeches, gauntlets and sword slings. While they are drying, he cleans the leather pieces and ends with the steels and brasses. It may take as long as from four to six hours.

85

The final touches to the wax model of Lady Diana at Madame Tussaud's. The day after the Wedding the model, made by Muriel Pearson, wore a replica of the Wedding dress made specially for Madame Tussaud's by the Emanuels themselves.

One of the Lady Diana car wave gimmicks – a danger on the road!

The trooper's basic kit is extensive. Each squadron has 109 horses, 96 of which are black, six greys, five chargers for the officers and two drum horses. The steel sword costs about £50 and the steel breastplate or cuirass more than three times as much. A cuirass has not been worn in battle since the seventeenth century, but since the 1930s it has been made of chromium to save polishing the steel.

Of the two regiments of the Household Cavalry, the Life Guards, who were raised in 1660, wear scarlet tunics and cloaks, white helmet plumes and white sheepskins. The Royal Horse Guards, now part of the Blues and Royals, were raised in 1661. In 1969 they amalgamated with the Royal Dragoons to form the Blues and Royals. They wear blue tunics and cloaks, red plumes and black sheepskins.

The announcement of the royal engagement was the signal for what amounted to an industry to spring up in Britain. Firms rushed into production with commemorative souvenirs of all kinds, and though the Lord Chamberlain's Office laid down guidelines, and the Design Centre chose certain items for approval, some of the results were amazing!

Some of the many Charles and Diana wedding souvenirs on sale.

There was an immediate boom in the sale of the Union Jack, and in the last weeks it hung seemingly everywhere. The first engagement photographs were very widely copied on pictures, postcards, tea towels, mugs, jigsaws, balloons and car stickers. It was as if the whole manufacturing industry, particularly of small items, was in full production. Gradually, the major companies, especially those in the fine china and glass fields, offered their range from collectors' items to the more common plates, mugs and thimbles. There were fountain pens, magazines mushroomed and the Mint offered crown pieces. Special souvenir shops appeared, particularly in London, offering a wide selection of almost everything from badges, dishes, clocks, albums, egg cosies, glassware, pin-cushions, scarves, moneyboxes, lovespoons (traditionally a symbol of betrothal in Wales), jewellery, even milk-bottle tops to silverware and gold pieces.

The Royal School of Needlework designed kneelers, and there were cushions and pictures embroidered on canvas. Jewellers were quick to make 'copies' of the engagement ring, and many cars had stickers on

*Right: Lord Brocket (on the left)
entertains American ladies, mainly
from Dallas, at Brocket Hall, one of
three stately homes where they stayed
as part of a ten-day Royal Wedding trip
which included Ascot, polo at Windsor
and a ball at the Savoy. The highlight of
the trip was, of course, seats along the
processional route on the day of the
wedding.*

*Below: A special Royal Wedding
beer named Dianamite being
brewed.*

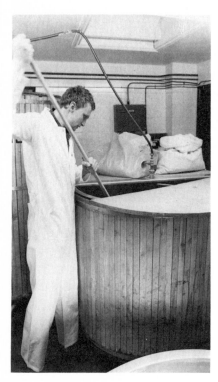

*Right: Happy tourists on the Lady
Diana coach tour outside her former
London home.*

them, or models of the Prince or Lady Diana 'waving' which proved very disconcerting on motorways!

Brewers all over the country had special beer and special labels, and the wine makers were not slow in offering a royal vintage to drink the health of the bride and groom. A housing scheme in London was named Althorp Mews, and London Transport had a Royal Wedding Warrant and Royal Wedding tours past Buckingham Palace and down the Mall to St Paul's, while other organizations ran tours to Althorp. Hotels and restaurants offered festive menus, and the Design Centre held an exhibition of souvenirs from July to September. The Post Office issued commemorative 14p and 25p stamps bearing a photograph of the Prince and Lady Diana taken by Lord Snowdon.

Ten royal occasions had already been celebrated with commemorative stamps since 1935 when stamps for the Silver Jubilee of King George V were issued. Others include the Coronation, the Investiture of Prince Charles, the silver wedding of the Queen, Princess Anne's wedding, the Silver Jubilee and the Queen Mother's eightieth birthday. Seventy other countries issued a series of stamps showing the Prince as 'Man of Action', others with flowers or Lady Diana, and many of the Prince in military and naval uniforms. There were first-day covers in the Seychelles, Anguilla and other Commonwealth countries, and a stamp company was set up in London to deal exclusively with the stamp boom.

A children's street party in Oxford Street, London, to celebrate the Royal Wedding.

91

The Royal Wedding

Prince Charles at an exhibition of handicapped children's skills coming face to face with look-alike pictures.

For weeks the whole country had been preparing in different ways to celebrate the Wedding. Schools had projects in which children made friezes and drawings or re-enacted the scene in dramatic sketches. Many were given commemorative mugs. Street parties, a great feature of the Silver Jubilee celebrations, were organized, and television manufacturers experienced a boom in colour sets. The day was a national holiday, and thousands travelled to London to be there on the day. The streets of the capital were gaily decorated, and hundreds booked space in office windows along the route to get a good view.

It was four months since the large white gilt-edged invitations with the words, 'The Lord Chamberlain is commanded by The Queen and The Duke of Edinburgh to invite . . .' had been sent out, and gradually the guests began to arrive in London. There were more than one hundred and sixty European royalty, Presidents, Prime Ministers and their wives from all over the world.

From the first announcement of the engagement the letters and presents had arrived at the Palace in shoals, and extra staff had to be called in to deal with them. It was decided that an exhibition of some of the presents in aid of charity would be set up in St James's Palace for several weeks after the Wedding. People came in their thousands to see the gifts which had been sent from all over the world and from all manner of people. Many came from individuals, especially children to whom Lady Diana had instantly endeared herself. There were 'sacrificial' gifts of their own treasures,

Left: A clown providing the entertainment at one of the many celebration street parties.

Below: Lady Diana pays a visit to the Young England Kindergarten and receives a posy from some young admirers.

things they had made in school or on their own, simple good luck messages from people genuinely anxious to show their affection. And there were the presents from regiments associated with the Prince, companies, councils (Sedgemoor gave a ton of peat for the garden, and Tetbury a new pair of gates for Highgrove House), and the Lord Mayor, Aldermen and Commons of the City of London gave a mahogany table and fourteen chairs.

There were three pianos, musical instruments, records, books, maps, glassware, bedlinen, charms, toys and gifts made by the donors with loving care. The people of Gosport sent loyal greetings delivered by thirty-three relay runners to raise money for the disabled. Navy reminders for the Prince included models and pictures of HMS *Bronington* in which he had served, and there was a poignant remembrance of his great-uncle, with the gift of the last car standard flown by Lord Mountbatten as Viceroy of India.

Jewellery, practical gifts, sporting presents (with the accent on horsy items) mingled with toffees, four-leafed clovers, soap and a record of the song 'Diana'. All bore testimony to the real love and affection in which the Prince and Lady Diana are held.

Gifts from the Royal Family and from other monarchs, as well as many from heads of state, were not on show, nor listed in the catalogue

A section of the Royal Wedding presents on show at St James's Palace.

*Above and left: More Wedding
gifts make a lavish display in aid
of charity.*

95

Above: A section of the Royal Mews at Buckingham Palace.

Left: Mrs Nancy Reagan, wife of the President of the United States of America, arriving in London for the Royal Wedding.

Opposite page, above: Jim Butler cleaning the carriage to be used by the bride and groom on the Royal Wedding Day.

Opposite page, below: Two footmen on the Glass Coach that is to take the bride to the Cathedral.

of gifts. As Prince Charles mentioned in his introduction to the list of gifts on show, 'many were not easily displayed', and many included gifts to charities 'which had been so much appreciated by the recipients'.

Special space had to be put aside at Buckingham Palace to store and list the gifts that were sent in a most moving token of love and good wishes on the occasion of the Royal Wedding.

The royal carriages and coaches are on display in the Royal Mews at Buckingham Palace when not in use. On the Wedding Day the first carriage procession would be for members of the Royal Family, followed by the Queen and then the bridegroom, each accompanied by an escort of the Household Cavalry. The beautiful Glass Coach built in 1910 and purchased by King George V for his Coronation was the one in which Lady Diana would ride with her father Earl Spencer from Clarence House to St Paul's, drawn by a pair of bay horses and with an escort of mounted police.

Prince Charles would ride in the 1902 State Postillion Landau built for Edward VII, accompanied by his supporter and brother Prince Andrew.

This would be drawn by four grey postillion horses in brass-mounted State harness with the special silver mane dressing prepared for the Queen's Silver Jubilee in 1977. After the service the Prince and Princess of Wales would return in the same landau.

The Queen and the Duke of Edinburgh would be driven in an open semi-state landau, one of five in the Royal Mews and drawn by four greys.

After the service two of the bridesmaids and the pages would return to the Palace in the Glass Coach used by the bride, and Prince Edward would accompany the other three bridesmaids in Queen Alexandra's State Coach. Prince Andrew would accompany his grandmother the Queen Mother. The Queen would ride with Earl Spencer, and the Duke of Edinburgh with Mrs Shand Kydd, mother of the bride.

The carriages and landaus would be driven by coachmen with postillions and footmen in State liveries, except for the bridegroom's, who would wear Ascot liveries.

The celebrations started after the weekend, and thousands enjoyed the spectacle of the firework display on the Wedding eve in Hyde Park. The weather was warm and sunny, and all along the Mall and in the parks the happy people – young and old alike – camped out so as not to miss their places. People had come from all over the world for the occasion, and London was bursting at the seams.

Below: Earl Spencer at St Paul's for the final Wedding rehearsal.

Dress was 'full colour with red, white and blue predominating', topped by 'funny' hats, rosettes, look-alike pictures of the couple and T-shirts the favourite garb of all ages and both sexes. Thousands spent a night under the stars, and as soon as the birds were astir on The Day, the crowds took up their positions. No one minded the long wait that lay ahead. Troops took their places to line the route and were cheered as they marched to their positions. The police were out in strength, but the whole atmosphere was good-natured and happy, as if it was 'their' day too, and everyone wanted to make the most of it. The streets were sanded to prevent the horses slipping, there was a bustle and a jingle of horse trappings and a tremendous air of excitement. Everyone knew it was going to be a perfect day, and their cheers would echo across the world, for they had come to show their love and admiration for the Prince of Wales and his bride, and nothing would stop them. Wedding fever was infectious, but no one minded the disease. It was going to be a day to remember.

The Duchess of Kent and Prince Edward leaving St Paul's Cathedral behind Prince Charles and Lady Diana after a Wedding rehearsal.

The Wedding

29 July 1981 was a lovely day in every sense of the word. The sun shone, the streets of London were ablaze with colour and excitement – indeed, the whole country was decorated with flags and bunting, and the whole world was watching the event.

The youthful Prince of Wales had pledged himself to the service of his country at his Investiture at Caernarvon in 1969, and, by his marriage to Lady Diana Spencer on this summer day, he dedicated himself anew, this time with his young bride at his side. It was an occasion in which everyone could play their part and express their delight, from those in high office who had worked so tirelessly to ensure that the ceremonial was perfection, and those who with infinite patience had hand-sewn much of the beautiful dress of the bride, to those who composed music for the occasion, all sending their affectionate good wishes with every action.

It was a crisp sparkling summer morning with a promise of warmth to come, setting the tone of sunny happiness for the new beginnings of their future lives together: a time of hope and anticipation in which, it seemed, the whole world wanted to share.

For those with stamina, after all-night (and in some cases more than one night's) vigils, there were good vantage points to be taken up. Some

Sun-tanned wellwishers preparing for a night in the open so as to be in prime positions for The Day.

elected to wait by Buckingham Palace to see the departures, and others crowded the steps and the approaches to St Paul's Cathedral to be there when everyone arrived and the first to see the newly-weds.

The whole of the processional route with its normally busy wide streets was lined with members of the armed services and police force who had taken up their positions at an early hour. Behind them the pavements were thronged with excited crowds in high good humour.

Outside the gates of Buckingham Palace the Society of Toastmasters carried out one of the habitual functions on special public occasions. Repeating their action on the occasion of the eightieth birthday of the Queen Mother, they stood resplendent in their traditional scarlet coats and held a public toast to the bride and groom.

The route led down the Mall, its red surface denoting its royal status, past Clarence House, home of the Queen Mother, where Lady Diana was

Early in the morning Royal Marines take up their position near Trafalgar Square.

staying. Outside there were specially large crowds hoping to catch a glimpse of her as she set out on her journey through the London streets.

Her carriage, following a short way behind the others, would take her into Trafalgar Square where Nelson's everseeing eye would watch her progress down the Strand, the Aldwych, past the Law Courts and into Fleet Street, then up Ludgate Hill to the Cathedral standing tall and magnificent in the sunshine.

The roadways, empty of people, except those scurrying across in the vain hope of a better vantage point further on, were sanded in readiness for the horses pulling the carriages and those of the escorts.

At 10 am the heads of the services left the Palace to inspect their men all along the route and ensure all was in order, for everything had to be perfect.

At the Cathedral the cars were pulling up with clockwork precision, bringing Kings and Queens, Presidents, Prime Ministers, lords and ladies, official guests, celebrities, the designers of the wedding dress, Lady Diana's hairdresser, the staff from all the royal homes specially invited, the three former flatmates of the bride, soon to sit in the front row of the vast congregation. This afforded much enlivening interest for the crowds, and cheers went up as each car unloaded its occupants, with special warmth for anyone they recognized.

Four former Prime Ministers, Mr Edward Heath, Lord Home, Sir Harold Wilson and Mr James Callaghan, among the congregation in the Cathedral.

103

Right: A procession of some of the crowned heads attending the Royal Wedding.

Lady Sarah McCorquodale, sister of the bride, at St Paul's.

The march past of the last Guards detachment to take up position along the route with the massed bands in order and the mounted escorts in formation was an indication that all was ready.

To the wildly increasing cheers of the crowds the royal processions clattered out of Buckingham Palace with their escorts from the Household Cavalry. The Duke and Duchess of Kent, Prince and Princess Michael of Kent, Princess Alexandra and the Hon. Angus Ogilvy, the Duke and Duchess of Gloucester, Princess Anne and Captain Mark Phillips, Princess Margaret, the Queen Mother and the Queen and Prince Philip moved along the Mall in a gay cavalcade. Finally, the moment they had all been waiting for as the Prince of Wales appeared, wearing the uniform of a Commander RN, accompanied by his supporter and brother Prince Andrew, in the uniform of a Midshipman RN, with the ring. His other supporter Prince Edward was escorting their grandmother the Queen Mother. Their landau left the Palace at 10.30 am taking the Prince on his last journey as a bachelor to St Paul's Cathedral.

Seven state landaus conveyed members of the Royal Family, and another the members of the Queen's and the Duke of Edinburgh's staff, with members of his personal staff behind the bridegroom.

Inside the Cathedral it was as if everyone bore witness to the first line of the poem specially composed by the Poet Laureate Sir John Betjeman for the Wedding:

'Let's all in love and friendship
hither come,'

and its ending couplet:

'And all of those assembled here
Are joyful in the love you share'.

In every sense it was a happy 'family' occasion, and not only for the families of the bride and bridegroom – it was as if the whole nation felt 'our' Prince was marrying 'one of us': the feeling of the citizens' possession was very marked.

Above: The Queen and Prince Philip on their way to St Paul's along a route lined with cheering enthusiastic crowds.

Left: Prince Edward, one of the supporters, accompanies his grandmother the Queen Mother to St Paul's.

The Cathedral was spotless. Before the guests arrived, cleaners had been at work giving a last vacuum to the great carpets, and everything sparkled.

The Queen and the Duke of Edinburgh turned and waved to the crowds from the doorway of the Cathedral, then entered to be greeted by the Archbishop of Canterbury, wearing a new blue and silver cope and mitre for the occasion. Preceded by the eighteen senior members of the Royal Family, including the Queen Mother, the Lord Mayor holding aloft the Pearl Sword given to the City of London by Elizabeth I, the Lord Steward and the Lord Chamberlain, and followed by the members of the Royal Household, they took their seats, and the Queen smilingly acknowledged the members of the bride's family sitting opposite.

The bridegroom arrived and preceded by two Admirals, acting as Gentleman Ushers, the Prince of Wales and his brothers, who were acting as his supporters, took their places, followed by members of his staff. The relaxed Prince smiled at friends he recognized during his long walk to his place on the raised platform specially erected for the day.

Clarence House was a bustle of activity. Everyone including the bride had been astir early, and after the ministrations of her hairdresser and

The Queen, with the Queen Mother, waving from the steps of the Cathedral.

Opposite page: To loud cheers Prince Charles leaves Buckingham Palace with his brother and supporter Prince Andrew, who carries the ring.

The veiled figure of Lady Diana accompanied by her father travelling in the Glass Coach with an escort of mounted police.

make-up artist and with help from the dressmakers and her mother and sisters, Lady Diana Spencer was ready for her marriage to the Prince of Wales.

The Glass Coach, with its escort of mounted civilian and military police, was ready to take her on her last journey as a commoner before she became the third lady in the land.

There were gasps and cheers and shouts of good wishes as the coach rumbled through the gateway, and the watchers caught a fleeting glimpse of the smiling and veiled bride, her father at her side. Her carriage left five minutes after that of her husband-to-be. Like his, her journey was filled with the cheers of the thousands lining the route and must have given her a feeling of confidence. The sound penetrated the Cathedral where Prince Charles was awaiting her arrival.

No one will forget the moment Lady Diana alighted from her coach and the full glory of her dress was revealed for the first time. With help from the chief bridesmaid Lady Sarah Armstrong-Jones, who had been bridesmaid to her sister Lady Sarah Spencer, the train was spread over the

*Prince Andrew and Prince Charles
entering the Cathedral.*

steps, and the bride turned as if to assure herself all was well before
mounting the steps on the arm of her father. The 25 ft-long (over 7.5 m)
train seemed to roll down the red carpeted steps of the Cathedral in an
ivory cascade, and the veil billowed out behind her in a cloud of tulle.

Inside, the designers were there to make final adjustments. A fanfare of
trumpets greeted her, and Lady Diana began to make the three and a half
minute walk along the longest royal red carpet ever installed, more than
650 ft (200 m) in length, to the accompaniment of the 'Trumpet
Voluntary'.

Lady Diana remained veiled which was a recent innovation for royal
brides. It is believed that Queen Victoria was the first English bride to
wear a veil. Hers was worn so as not to conceal her face, a tradition kept up
by succeeding brides until Princess Anne changed the custom in 1973. She
wore a long veil over her face during her marriage.

Lady Diana's dress was a combination of many things – romance,
enchantment, Victorian, Edwardian, even Tudor designs, but perfect for
her. The beautiful ivory silk taffeta crinoline shimmered in the sunlight as

Lady Diana's long train is arranged on the steps as she goes into the Cathedral on the arm of her father.

it danced on the embroidery. The lace-trimmed sleeves were ruffled with matching bows. Ten thousand mother-of-pearl sequins and pearls with a tiny diamond-encrusted gold horseshoe stitched among them for luck gave a radiance to the soft flowing featherweight silk as she moved. Her veil was held in place by the Spencer tiara, and she had 'borrowed' diamond earrings from her mother. A flounce of antique Carrick-ma-Cross lace, presented to the Royal School of Needlework by Queen Mary, formed lace panels on the dress. Her shoes were ivory silk with fluted heels and pointed toes and a heart-shaped decoration in front. To prevent her slipping, the soles were specially sueded.

The bride's structured shower bouquet by Longmans was of Mountbatten roses, lily-of-the-valley, white freezias, stephanotis, white orchids and trailing ivy leaves. The traditional myrtle and veronica from bushes grown from some cuttings from Queen Victoria's wedding bouquet were included. After the service the bouquet was laid, in keeping

Opposite page: A long view of the bride's procession up the aisle.

Below: The congregation singing the first hymn.

Left: Prince Charles placing the ring on Lady Diana's finger.

Opposite page: The Archbishop of Canterbury pronouncing the Blessing.

Left: Prince Charles and Lady Diana exchange a word during the service.

with a royal tradition started by the Queen Mother after her wedding in 1923, on the Tomb of the Unknown Warrior in Westminster Abbey.

The bridesmaids' dresses were in a style that echoed, but did not exactly copy, that of the bride. The colour and feeling were there, but hemlines varied. Their headdresses were crowns of fresh flowers, and the older ones carried posies and the small children baskets of flowers, so they resembled an illustration from a Victorian story-book. And the page boys, in naval cadet uniforms of 1863, were the perfect finishing touch.

There was a reassuring smile for the bride as she reached the Prince's side. The congregation sang the opening hymn, and the Cathedral was hushed for the solemnization of matrimony. The couple made their vows clearly though Lady Diana transposed two of her husband's Christian names, and he omitted a word from his vows. They knelt and were blessed by the Archbishop. Lord Spencer, his duty of giving away his youngest daughter done, was assisted to his seat by his son. His courage and determination throughout the long day won him the admiration of all.

The bride and groom listened to the Lesson, the specially composed Anthem and the address by the Archbishop before moving up to the altar for the prayers. Everyone joined in the last hymn, 'I vow to thee, my

Left: During the signing of the register, Miss Kiri Te Kanawa sang an aria from Samson.

Below: The signatures of bride and groom in the register.

Opposite page: A solemn moment at the altar for the bride and groom.

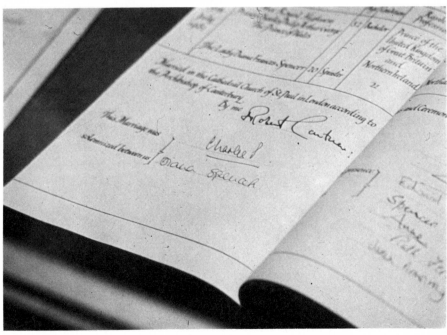

117

Right: The Prince bows and the Princess curtseys to the Queen.

Opposite page: The Prince and Princess of Wales walk smiling to the main door.

country', which became a symbolic undertaking from everyone. The couple knelt once more for the final blessing by the Archbishop, and the National Anthem in its new setting by David Willcocks was sung with fervour.

The Archbishop led the Prince and Princess through the sanctuary gates into the south aisle with Lady Sarah Armstrong-Jones, the senior bridesmaid, close behind. The Dean of St Paul's conducted the Queen and Prince Philip followed by members of both families for the signing of the register. While this was being done an aria and chorus from Handel's oratorio *Samson* was sung by the New Zealand soprano Kiri Te Kanawa and the Bach Choir.

The Royal Family and the bride's family then resumed their seats. An exultant fanfare played by the State Trumpeters in the Whispering Gallery heralded the return of the bride and groom. It was a moment of sheer beauty as the Princess of Wales, her veil turned back, revealed her radiant, tremulously shy face.

Prince Charles bowed to the Queen, and the Princess of Wales curtseyed low. After smiling at her mother, they faced the congregation

together for the first time and walked to the door to the wonderfully stirring and very English music of Elgar's *Pomp and Circumstance* March No. 4 in G.

The service was over, and with it an unforgettable hour in which a young couple had pledged themselves in marriage before the watching eyes of the world. As with all marriages, it was a time of new beginnings, and it brought a breath of fresh air to a jaded country. The time-honoured service had a new meaning, the music and singing were unsurpassed, and everyone from the trumpeters in the Whispering Gallery to the orchestras, the organists, the choirs (which included for the first time a lady taperer) had played their parts in the fabric of the whole wonderful happening.

For a moment, the Prince and Princess of Wales paused on the steps of St Paul's as they emerged into the sunlight and the deafening volume of cheering that awaited their appearance.

With happy smiles the newly married couple moved down the red carpet together, past the stepliners representing those services, ships and regiments with which the Prince had served or had connections, and, after a little adjustment to the train, climbed into the landau to begin the long drive to Buckingham Palace. The vehicle had been specially decorated with the gift of a gold horseshoe for luck from the staff of the Royal Mews and a posy of flowers.

Church bells pealed all over London, and the cheers reverberated everywhere. Progress was slow, but no one minded as long as they caught sight of Prince Charles and his beautiful wife. The Queen returned with Earl Spencer beside her, smiling and waving to acknowledge the applause that greeted her. The Duke of Edinburgh escorted the bride's mother Mrs Shand Kydd in another carriage, but inevitably all eyes were on the bride

Opposite page: A moment's pause on the threshold for the bride and groom to absorb the cheers that awaited them.

Below: With a little help from her husband, the Princess climbs into the carriage.

121

The newly-weds wave to the crowds on their way back to Buckingham Palace.

and groom, both looking radiantly happy on this their special day.

Fittingly for a naval officer, sailors lined the route as the bridal carriage rounded Trafalgar Square and turned into the last straight red road where Buckingham Palace awaited them at the end.

The crowds were almost overwhelming with their cheers, everyone anxious to show their true feelings. At last the landau with the waving and happily smiling Prince and Princess reached the comparative peace of the Palace and disappeared from sight. Immediately, the chants began, 'We want the Prince and Princess', and then more vociferously, 'We want Charles and Diana' in an insistent quickening rhythm, getting louder and louder as time went on.

After the Queen's and the other royal processions had returned to Buckingham Palace, the crowds broke ranks, and the whole Mall became a human tide, a mosaic of people that was incredible to watch as it swayed and moved with a curious dancing motion.

Finally the Prince and Princess emerged through the glass doors on to the balcony, and the cheers rose to new heights. The crowd would not let them go and started singing a song often heard at football matches, 'You'll never walk alone', making it like a pledge. Again and again they appeared, and the other members of the Royal Family joined them, smiling and waving, with the bridesmaids peeping over the edge in bewilderment.

*Above: Prince Philip and
Mrs Shand Kydd on their way
back to the Palace.*

*Left: The Queen and Earl Spencer
leave St Paul's.*

Above: The bride and groom nearing Buckingham Palace on their triumphal journey.

Right: Princess Anne and Princess Margaret return to Buckingham Palace.

At last came the moment they had all been clamouring for. The Prince gallantly kissed his bride's hand, and then, for the first time, he kissed her for all the world to see. For the crowds it was the final rapture, and their delight knew no bounds.

To the groans and shouts of protest of the crowd, now reluctant to let them go for a minute, the bride and groom gave a last wave and went inside to receive their guests, and the doors shut.

Still savouring that perfect moment, the crowds mused and laughed and waited. They *knew* the Prince and his beautiful Princess would not disappoint them. There would be another appearance. There *had* to be.

Inside, the Queen's cousin, and top photographer, Lord Lichfield, had been commissioned to take the wedding photographs. For days he had been trying the lighting and deciding how to achieve the best angles and groupings.

The perfection of this collection was revealed later with the publication of the pictures. Obviously the Prince and Princess were the stars, but Patrick Lichfield had managed to convey an air of complete naturalness in them that was a rarity, especially in such a setting and with such subjects. The Prince and Princess stood smiling, this way and that, with and

Above: The smiling Prince and Princess wave to the crowds from the balcony.

Overleaf: The traditional family group on the Palace balcony with the bride and bridegroom, bridesmaids, pages, the Queen and Prince Philip, the Queen Mother, Ruth Lady Fermoy, Prince Andrew, Prince Edward, Earl Spencer and the Hon. Mrs Shand Kydd.

Right: A close-up of the pretty slippers worn by the Princess of Wales. Nestling in the top is her garter.

Below: The Royal Family Wedding group of 1981. The Prince and Princess of Wales with their attendants, the Royal Family, the bride's family and the crowned heads of the royal families who had come to England for the Wedding — Belgium, Norway, Denmark, Sweden, The Netherlands, Luxembourg, Lichtenstein and Monaco — photographed at Buckingham Palace.

The kiss that was the climax of the balcony scenes.

without the attendants and supporters. A lovely study of the Princess alone with her beautiful bouquet and the full magnificence of her dress and train arranged around her, and the unusual shot of the Prince leaning to kiss his wife's hand, were unforgettable.

Perhaps the most amusing of all was the one of the bride and groom with the bridesmaids and pages in a heap of clothes and legs on the floor! Apparently Lord Lichfield had told them all to relax, and after the events of the tiring morning they did. It made a wonderful photograph.

As with every wedding, there were the inevitable family groups, but there was a final one that was different that day. To begin with there were fifty-seven people in this group, Kings and Queens of Europe, the Royal Family, the bride's family, the bride and groom and attendants. It was a problem for the photographer to assemble and keep the pose while they

Opposite page: The smiling Prince and Princess.

Below: A happy, relaxed moment of informality caught by Lord Lichfield.

all took their allotted place. There could hardly be 'retakes' with such a gathering! Patrick Lichfield had a unique solution. He arranged everyone by numbered places, and while they stood talking he waited until they were all in place and then blew a whistle to call them to order. The photograph was a masterpiece: the official photographer at Buckingham Palace on this great day had surpassed himself.

An hour after their first appearance, to the delight and approval of the dense crowds who stood chanting, a heaving happy mob, the Prince and the Princess of Wales with the Duke of Edinburgh and the Queen, made another balcony appearance to acknowledge the cheers and wave to the people gathered in ranks stretching as far as the eye could see.

The bride and bridegroom were now able to entertain the 120 guests, their relatives and closest friends to the wedding breakfast in the Ball Supper Room. The cake was cut with the Prince's ceremonial sword, the toasts drunk and the family party relaxed for a while.

The next time the Prince and Princess of Wales appeared to the public it was to start their honeymoon.

The Honeymoon

At four o'clock the word went round that the Prince and Princess of Wales were about to leave on their honeymoon, to the delight of the now hot, dusty but happy crowds.

The television viewers scored here for they could see into the Palace itself and watch the crowds of family, friends and staff gathering round the entrance. The carriage and escort were drawn up, this time with a difference, for a cluster of large blue and silver balloons, each bearing Prince of Wales feathers, were tied in a bunch at the back, gently swaying in the breeze. A large handwritten placard complete with hearts and arrows said it all: 'Just Married'.

At last, to cheers and cries of delight, the Prince and Princess emerged. He was now wearing a lounge suit and his bride looked stunning in a coral pink suit and five-string pearl choker, with a perky little hat swathed in ostrich feathers.

The carriage moved through the archway to the cheers and waves of the Royal Family who, like any other family, had come to see them off. They were showered with rose petals and confetti as they left the Palace on the start of their honeymoon.

The carriage drove round the familiar streets of London, still lined with waving and cheering crowds, to Waterloo Station, the new Princess serene and happy, and her husband clearly delighted.

Below left: A close-up of the balloons with Prince of Wales feathers and the 'JUST MARRIED' sign on the back of the carriage.

Below right: The Prince and Princess in their carriage on their way to Waterloo.

Waterloo Station was *en fête* with the traditional red carpet laid on Platform 12 in front of the special three-carriage royal train that would take them to Romsey to spend two days at Broadlands before setting out on the next stage of their honeymoon.

British Rail officials greeted the royal couple, and the Lord Chamberlain, who had been in charge of the wedding arrangements, was rewarded with a kiss from the Princess as she climbed into the train. Another wave, and the train rumbled out of the station on its way to the small Hampshire town of Romsey.

The eighty-mile journey was swiftly accomplished, and the Prince and Princess of Wales emerged to another welcome at Romsey. It seemed as if the whole flag-waving, cheering population had turned out to greet them, swelled by a mass of sightseers and the inevitable press corps.

Broadlands was only a mile away, but the dense crowds and the force of their enthusiasm made it a slow ride. At last the royal car slipped gently through the gates, and at the Hampshire home of the late Lord Louis Mountbatten, where the Queen and Prince Philip had spent their first days of married life in 1947, Prince Charles and his Princess began their new life together.

The six thousand acre estate with its eighteenth-century mansion overlooking the River Test was secluded, and the newly-weds had a couple of days' peace before, on the afternoon of Saturday 1 August, they left once more to the cheers of the crowds and were driven to Eastleigh Airport to fly in an Andover of the Queen's Flight to Gibraltar.

The sparkling sunshine of Gibraltar made a perfect background for the Princess's filmy flowery dress, and the people of the colony made every

The newly-weds at Westminster Bridge on their way to Waterloo Station at the start of their honeymoon.

133

Opposite page: Jubilant crowds welcome the royal honeymooners in Gibraltar.

Right: The Princess shaking hands on her arrival at Broadlands in Hampshire.

Above: A wave from the Princess as she boards the honeymoon train.

Right: The Prince and Princess waving from their aircraft as they leave for Gibraltar to join the royal yacht.

Overleaf: Britannia and escort at Gibraltar.

135

Right: A delightful honeymoon picture on board Britannia.

Right: The Princess of Wales in a stunningly simple pink outfit being welcomed with Prince Charles in Egypt.

138

effort to make them welcome. Bunting, flags, all conceivable decorations hung from the balconies of houses, and the streets were lined by thousands of excited eager people wishing them well. It was only a short drive to the docks where the royal yacht *Britannia* lay at anchor, but a memorable one.

The quayside was soon awash with cameramen, and the smiling couple posed time and again to try to satisfy the insatiable demand for more pictures. One of the most endearing was a hand-in-hand shot as they walked the deck together before the ship sailed. Their brief visit to the Rock of Gibraltar over, the royal yacht left her moorings and sailed out of the harbour, a flotilla of small boats in escort, to the accompaniment of sirens and the echoes of the cheers.

Britannia, launched in 1954, has a crew of twenty-two officers and about two hundred and fifty men. She can best be described as a floating palace, designed specially for the Sovereign's use when on overseas tours, and is beautifully equipped from her royal blue hull to her snow-white superstructure. In time of war she can be converted into a hospital ship. With true regal frugality, items from earlier royal yachts have been incorporated into the fittings, including a gimbal table designed by Prince Albert and a binnacle from the Prince Regent's *Royal George*.

The idyllic voyage continued on the sunny Mediterranean with much speculation as to the eventual destination. But the ship's course was a secret, though it was claimed the honeymooners picnicked in remote inlets on the North African coasts and enjoyed barbecues on beaches in the Greek islands.

One stop was certain. The royal yacht docked at Port Said where they were officially received by the late President of Egypt, Anwar Sadat, and his wife Jihan. The Prince inspected a Guard of Honour, and a hatless sun-tanned Princess in a soft pink dress talked with the President's wife. That evening the Egyptian visitors were the guests of the Prince and Princess aboard the royal yacht, and in true naval tradition the Royal Marines band played for 'Sunset' on shore alongside the ship.

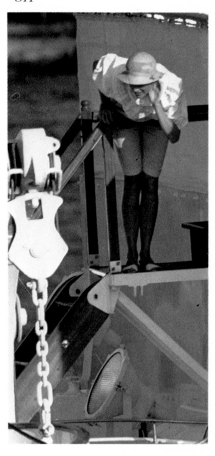

An informal photograph and yet another fashion setter! The Princess in Bermuda shorts arriving in Egypt.

Left: A sun-tanned Prince and Princess with the late President Sadat and Mrs Sadat on board Britannia.

139

Right: The Princess of Wales flying into London from Scotland on a surprise visit to Highgrove.

Below: The photographers who gathered at Balmoral.

140

Since his student days at Cambridge, the Prince has had a keen interest in archaeology, and it had been hoped it might be possible to visit some of the treasures of Egypt on this visit. However, next day the ship sailed through the Suez Canal and docked on the Egyptian Red Sea coast for a last bathe in the blue waters before the Royal honeymooners flew back to Scotland from an Egyptian military airfield.

After the relentless heat of an Egyptian sun, Scotland was cold on arrival, and the smiling Princess wore a long white cashmere coat as she landed at Lossiemouth.

The honeymoon was not over, and the Prince and his bride drove to Balmoral for a few weeks' holiday before taking up official duties once more.

Much had to be done: there were more presents to see and acknowledge and visits to plan, and the Princess took time to fly to London and Highgrove in Gloucestershire to assure herself that the alterations and renovations for their new homes were going well.

The media were never far away, and the royal couple graciously agreed to pose for photographs on the beautiful hillside near Balmoral. The Prince was, as is usual for the Royal Family while in Scotland, wearing a kilt, and the Princess looked relaxed and happy in a fetching check suit.

A relaxed royal couple pose for the media at Balmoral. The press presented the Princess with a bouquet.

Right: Wearing a checked outfit and black tam-o'-shanter the Princess, with other members of the Royal Family, was a welcome spectator at the Braemar Gathering.

Below right: The press presenting flowers to the Princess at Balmoral.

Above: The Princess of Wales leaving Crathie church after morning service.

When accepting a bouquet from the newsmen, she laughingly asked if it was 'on expenses' and said she 'thoroughly recommended marriage'.

For a time there was some privacy for the newly-weds, though thousands flocked to Crathie church in the hope of catching a glimpse of them when they, with other members of the Royal Family, attended morning service. All too soon royal duties intruded, and in the sixth week of the honeymoon the Prince and Princess accompanied other members of the Royal Family on their annual visit to the Braemar Gathering. It was to be the Princess's first public appearance in Scotland with her husband, and, perhaps as a compliment to that country, she wore a delightful Scottish plaid suit in burgundy topped with a large black tam-o'-shanter. It won her immediate acclaim as did her very real enjoyment of the traditional events of Scottish dancing, tossing the caber and others that go to make up such a happening.

Soon the honeymoon would be a memory, but the Princess had won many hearts with her beauty and charm, and there was a world waiting for her to meet and conquer in the months lying ahead.

142

A New Life

The lazy autumn days at Balmoral provided the tranquillity needed to plan for the taxing royal days that lay ahead. For the Princess, it would be a new and demanding role, for everyone was anxious to meet and welcome her, the new member of the Royal Family. There would be the public functions that already crowded the calendar and the additional burdens of settling into new homes, for the Prince and his bride had their private residence at Highgrove and their London residence at Kensington Palace.

It was a time of new beginnings and aspirations and, for the Princess, a chance to establish her own personality and style. As the woman married to the Heir to the Throne, her every move would be public property, and she would be expected to fulfil her full role in the royal pattern. Her love of children was well known, and her obvious sympathy was an endearing quality. As the third lady in the land there were many fields open to her, and whatever she chose would be of importance. In her own right she would become a leader and must tread with some caution.

Her predecessors had, in a different time and style, busied themselves with charitable works, and the Princess of Wales would probably be showered with invitations and requests for her patronage. Her innate kindness and ability to talk to anyone was a decided asset assuring her of a place in the nation's affections.

A view of the gardens at Highgrove. The house is only six miles from Gatcombe Park where Princess Anne lives with her husband Captain Mark Phillips and their children.

Lanning Roper, designer of the gardens at Highgrove. An American, he went to Princeton University School of Architecture and was a lieutenant-commander in the U.S. Navy during the war. He trained at Kew Gardens and Edinburgh Botanical Gardens.

The staff at Wolfscastle County Hotel, near Haverfordwest, toast Rosanna Lloyd on her appointment as cook-housekeeper at Highgrove.

In private, she was the wife of the Prince of Wales, and their personal life together must be carefully preserved.

Highgrove, the Gloucestershire home bought by Prince Charles, had been refurbished according to the couple's tastes and was ready for their occupation. The house was built for John Paul Paul between 1796 and 1798 on an estate once belonging to his maternal grandfather, Robert Clark. The 200-year-old mansion has an imposing entrance hall, more than 40 ft (12 m) in length, with a broad staircase leading up from it. The large reception rooms are on either side. There are four main bedrooms and bathrooms and the nursery suite on the first floor. The house contains many marble fireplaces, and the best of these, in the drawing room, is decorated with a carved dolphin which is the heraldic emblem of Tetbury.

Once the property of publisher and politician Maurice Macmillan, the house has nine bedrooms on the second floor, and outside there is some excellent stabling. The grounds are large, some 350 acres of woods and fields, offering seclusion, though it is within easy access of London. The first owners, the Pauls, were Huguenot immigrants who settled in the Cotswolds because of the cloth trade.

A later owner, William Yatman, presented Tetbury church with a new clock and chimes, and the rehanging of the bells was in memory of his son. He insisted that the view of the spire was kept free of trees as he liked to see it from the windows of the house. The view is kept clear to this day.

The formal garden contains a fine cedar of Lebanon and an avenue of golden yews, and the whole is gracious and gentle with soft country air. Special security precautions had to be installed, and a former estate cottage is now a police station. The Tetbury Council's wedding present to the couple was a pair of new gates for the main entrance, skilfully made by local blacksmith Hector Cole.

One sunny day large vans began unloading the furniture chosen by the Prince and Princess for their home, including many wedding presents. Soon the house was ready for occupation. To the delight of their neighbours, Highgrove House was another royal residence at last.

Left: The stables at Highgrove, with the horses in residence.

Below: Moving-in day at Highgrove.

Blacksmith Hector Cole making the new gates for Highgrove. These were the wedding gift from Tetbury Council to the royal couple.

The London home of the Prince and Princess is Kensington Palace where, surrounded by royal relatives and senior Court officials, they have a flat in the north-west wing.

Kensington Palace, in nearly 300 acres of Kensington Gardens, is in the heart of London, yet very rural in atmosphere. The peaceful gardens, where for more than a hundred years nannies have pushed their charges in prams, or sat and talked with their friends under the green plane trees, are a beautiful sight in midsummer. Prince Charles, often unnoticed, was pushed round these gardens as a baby and, like thousands before (and after) him, sailed his toy boat on the Round Pond.

Wrought iron railings just off the busy Kensington High Street give privacy to those who live in an almost 'village' community with little walled gardens and cobbled courtyards, often ablaze with summer flowers.

Kensington Palace, of mellowed red brick, has been Crown property since 1689, and was once the most loved home of the Sovereigns. Queen Victoria and Queen Mary were born there, and it is now the home of several members of the Royal Family.

William III suffered from asthma and, seeking a residence away from the dampness caused by the proximity of the river at Whitehall, purchased Nottingham House, as it was then called, in 1689. The name reverted to Kensington and alterations began under Sir Christopher Wren.

In later years George I, who felt the Palace reminded him of Herrenhausen in his beloved Hanover, made considerable alterations, rebuilding and creating the State Apartments, now open to the public.

Thirteen of George III's family lived to adulthood there, and his son the

Above: Kensington Palace, the London home of the Prince and Princess.

Left: An old print of Kensington Palace.

Above, top to bottom: The Princess's Ladies-in-Waiting, Miss Anne Beckwith-Smith, Mrs Hazel West and Mrs Lavinia Baring.

Right: Princess Alexandra soon after her marriage to the Prince of Wales, later Edward VII.

Duke of Kent occupied a suite on the east side where Queen Victoria was born in 1819. She was the last Sovereign to live in the Palace. More recently Prince Philip's grandmother, the Dowager Marchioness of Milford Haven, and Princess Marina lived there, and Princess Margaret and Prince and Princess Michael of Kent (who also have a country house in Gloucestershire) live there today.

Three floors at 8–9 Kensington Palace have been converted for the Prince and Princess of Wales. The Palace was extensively damaged by bombs in the Second World War, and it was not until 1975 that renovation work began, much to the interest of the Prince. He had dubbed the Palace the 'ants' nest' because of the number of his aunts who once lived there, and Princess Margaret's house was called the 'doll's house'. Later she moved to No. 1a with a walled garden. Restoration work took five years, and gradually the apartments took shape. A peaceful, paved quadrangle stretches out beneath the drawing room windows, known for centuries as 'Prince of Wales's Court'. It was named after Prince Frederick, son of George II, the cello-playing prince whose sister Princess Anne played the clavichord. Handel, Master of the King's Musick, arranged birthday and other celebration dances in the cloistered courtyard for their entertainment.

The Prince and Princess of Wales will be surrounded by family history in their London home. Thirty-four years ago, Prince Philip left for his marriage to the Queen from his grandmother's house door with the Kensington Palace sweep to wish him well. And there are the memories of the thirteen children of George III who grew up there and of the young Queen Victoria.

The progress of Princess Alexandra, Princess of Wales, through London in 1863.

The State Visit of the Prince and Princess of Wales to the Royal Italian Opera at Covent Garden in 1863.

Lady Jane Fellowes, sister of the Princess, lives 'just down the road' at a house called the Old Barracks, and nearly next door are the Duke and Duchess of Gloucester, with Princess Alexandra and Angus Ogilvy having an 'overnight' flat in the Palace.

So Kensington Palace is brimming with new young Royal life, a happy background for the new Princess of Wales to begin her private life with her husband and public life as a member of the Royal Family.

All around her the wheels of the Buckingham Palace organization have been set in motion with her personal staff on hand to assist. The appointment of the three Ladies-in-Waiting selected by the Princess was announced in late September. One, Miss Anne Beckwith-Smith, who worked at Sotheby's, would be full time, and the other two, Mrs Hazel West and Mrs Lavinia Baring, part time. Mrs West, the wife of Lieutenant-Colonel George West, Assistant Comptroller at the Lord Chamberlain's Office, where the Royal Wedding arrangements were made, already had some intimation of her task, but none had any actual experience of their new work.

Royal Ladies-in-Waiting are those who, almost unseen, provide the sympathy, support and strength for their royal mistress. They are aware of the difficulties facing a member of the Royal Family, and it is their role to smooth away the problems.

A Lady-in-Waiting has to accompany the Princess on official duties and act as companion and secretary on a rota system. It is hard, but rewarding work, and anyone appointed becomes a close friend of a member of the Family. The pay is nominal, but the lifestyle attractive, and they live outside the Palace. They have to dress well but quietly, remember the names and faces of those the Princess will meet and be prepared to cope with any emergency that may arise. A great sense of humour is a must, as well as remarkable stamina. A Lady-in-Waiting has an important role to play for she is the contact between the Princess and the public, and all too often the success or failure of an occasion depends on her organization.

The present Princess of Wales is the ninth in a line stretching back to Joan of Kent who married Edward, the Black Prince, in 1361. The title is only held by reason of marriage to a Prince of Wales, and no woman has ever held it in her own right.

Princess Alexandra of Denmark, wife of Edward VII, played an increasing role in public life during nearly thirty-eight years as Princess of Wales. The couple lived at Marlborough House in the Mall and had acquired Sandringham in Norfolk. With her husband enjoying every moment, they entertained lavishly and were the leaders of fun and fashion in late Victorian London.

Her first public visit to Wales was on 25 April 1868 when with the Prince of Wales she visited Caernarvon, travelling by special train. On arrival the Princess was presented with a bouquet and rode in an open carriage through the streets where 'every window was filled with human heads' and 'people cheered as though they would never tire of the exercise'.

At Caernarvon Castle the Prince and Princess posed for photographs in Queen Eleanor's gateway and were given an illuminated address. The

Presentation of an address from the people of North Wales to the Prince and Princess of Wales at Caernarvon Castle in 1868.

The Prince of Wales, later Edward VII, and the Princess of Wales.

Princess was given a 'gold medal of handsome design to commemorate her first visit to the Principality at Caernarvon, April 1868'. They toured the Castle apartments, and in the evening there was a huge banquet, at which the High Sheriff reminded the Prince and Princess that the first Prince of Wales born within the walls of the Castle had been born on that day, 25 April 1284, and their visit coincided with his birthday. He assured them of a warm welcome, and every building was illuminated.

Princess Alexandra was a skilled pianist and expert player on the mandoline, playing in an orchestra under the pseudonym of Countess Gage. She took a keen interest in music, especially the Royal College of Music, and Alexandra House, a hostel for students, was named after her. There was a custom that the students annually sent her a bouquet of white roses, and she attended many functions there.

The Princess took an active part in nursing work, and her many visits to hospitals brought a great deal of happiness. She was President of the London Hospital, at that time the largest in the world, and a statue was erected to her there. Her particular interest was the work of one of her countrymen into 'disease of the lupus' (a form of tuberculosis), and a special Finsen Ray Department was set up. Queen Alexandra's Royal Nursing Service bears her name as do many regiments in the British Army.

She is remembered for her work with orphan children, hospitals and the Soldiers' and Sailors' Families' Association. She was also Patron of Dr Barnardo's Homes and other orphanages. The sea was not forgotten in the Sailors' Homes of Dame Agnes Weston and training ships in the Thames such as the *Goliath* used for training boys from workhouse schools.

Perhaps her greatest memorial is that of Alexandra Day set up in 1912 as a flag day to raise funds for charity.

The next Princess of Wales was her daughter-in-law, Princess Mary of Teck, wife of the Duke of York (later King George V), whose life spanned more than eighty years and two world wars. The daughter of a German Duke of the House of Württemberg, her mother was grand-daughter of George III. She became betrothed to Prince Albert, Prince of Wales, but after his death in 1892 became engaged a year later to his brother Prince George, later Prince of Wales, and they married in 1893.

In 1901 the Duke and Duchess of York embarked on a world tour and on their return were given the title of the Prince and Princess of Wales. In 1902 the new Prince and Princess of Wales took their places at the State Opening of Parliament. She wore a long crimson ermine-lined train held by pages, and a girdle of diamonds round her waist reached to her knees.

The Prince and Princess of Wales enjoyed Society life in London with frequent visits to the theatre, and, an expert on interiors, she busied herself with re-arranging Marlborough House. They entertained many foreign royalties in England for the Coronation, and at the ceremony the Princess set a new fashion. Her ladies-in-waiting wore white satin dresses with a design of feathers in diamante all up the front and round the skirt.

A party at Frogmore in 1909 showing the Princess of Wales, later Queen Mary, and three of her children.

Right: Queen Mary talking to disabled ex-servicemen.

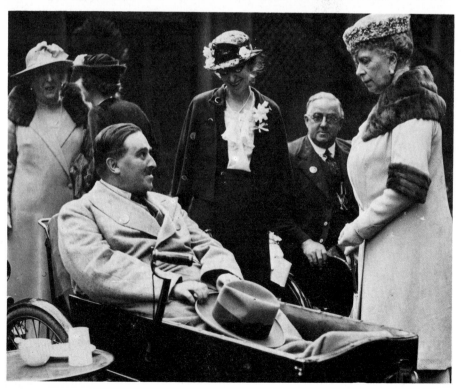

152

Queen Mary on her 80th birthday.

The Princess, later Queen Mary, took an active part in England's affairs and carried out many tours with dignity. In the First World War she visited hospitals in France and launched the Queen's Work for Women Fund which did invaluable work. She also organized needlework and knitting guilds all over the country. At Badminton House in the Second World War, she participated in many activities, not least the collecting of salvage. When men of the Gloucestershire Regiment were billeted in the stables as a guard for her, Queen Mary as mother of the regiment's Colonel-in-Chief, the Duke of Gloucester, wore their cap badge in her hat.

As the years passed, Queen Mary, by her tall regal figure and superb dignity, won the love and respect of all. Seemingly imperturbable, she bore great sorrows – the death of her husband and three sons and the Abdication of Edward VIII – with immense courage. Her compensations surely came in the reign of her grand-daughter and her pleasure in her great-grandson Prince Charles.

153

Prince Charles taking leave of his wife before flying to attend President Sadat's funeral.

Day One of the Welsh tour, at Deeside Leisure Centre, and the Princess of Wales's first official engagement since her marriage.

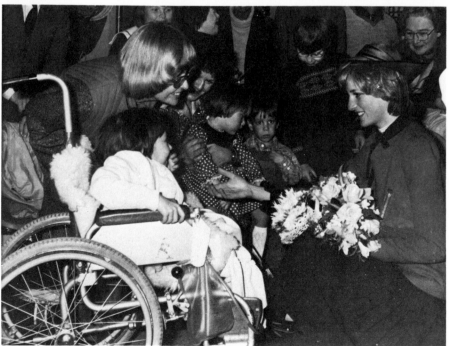

Opposite page: The Princess acknowledging the cheers of the people of Rhyl during her first Welsh visit.

The Princess of Wales making new friends on a royal walkabout in Wales.

Almost eighty years have passed since there has been a Princess of Wales, and the people of the Principality had been planning and arranging for the promised visit of the Prince and Princess of Wales in October 1981, a matter of weeks after their wedding.

In Scotland the Princess attended morning service at Crathie church near Balmoral and flew to London before the commencement of the royal tour of Wales.

The Prince and Princess travelled by royal train and car, arriving at the Royal Borough of Caernarvon at 3.20 in the afternoon to an enthusiastic welcome from the crowds who had waited hours to see their Princess.

In an attractive outfit of red and green, a thoughtful tribute to the Welsh national colours, the Princess lost no time in getting to know the Welsh people and was almost overwhelmed by all those wanting to shake her hand or give her bunches of flowers. An immediate rapport built up at once, and the word buzzed round, 'She's lovely! She's sympathetic to us', borne out by her exclamations of 'Poor you, my hands are cold too' when encountering an icy handshake.

The highlight of the visit was a walk round the age-old castle of Caernarvon, site of the Prince's Investiture in 1969. Sitting in the same slate seats on the state podium where the Prince was invested by the Queen, they listened to the singing of a choir of Welsh children. Lord Snowdon, Constable of the Castle, was there to welcome them as he had welcomed the Prince in July 1969.

Symbolically, they paused and looked down from the Queen's Gate at the throng below, as if the Prince was presenting his Princess to the people of Wales for approval. Their cheers gave him his answer.

Opposite page: The Princess of Wales receiving flowers from the crowds in Rhyl.

Overleaf: The Prince and Princess listening to a Welsh choir in Caernarvon Castle.

157

The Prince and Princess of Wales look down from a gallery in Caernarvon Castle.

The day started at Shotton, where they heard a recital by a Welsh harpist who had played for the Prince before his Investiture. Then on to Rhyl and Llandudno, ending the day at Caernarvon. As they drove away in their flower-filled car, the cheers echoing behind them, the Prince and Princess must have been heartened by the obvious delight of all who had seen them.

The second day of the Welsh visit was wet and cold, but the smiling Princess made light of it, and her beige coat and matching ostrich feather hat were to be seen everywhere, sometimes under an umbrella.

At St David's Cathedral the Prince and Princess attended the 800th anniversary service. Later, on the now familiar walkabouts, the Princess had some surprises. One man kissed her hand, and she was showered with presents and flowers. People held on to her hand so long and so hard that she was heard to beg for it back. But no one wanted to let her go, such was her fascination.

In Swansea, the oldest miner in Wales, a Mr Daniels, was presented to the Prince and Princess, and the 105-year-old man told them he 'remembered Prince Edward, Prince of Wales'.

The Prince announced to the delighted cheers of the crowds that the Queen had given permission to raise the status of the Mayor of Swansea to Lord Mayor.

*Left: Two policewomen at
St David's laden with flowers that
had been given to the Princess.*

*Below: The royal couple's
procession makes its way through
the crowded streets of
Haverfordwest.*

Day Three on the 400-mile-long tour of Wales was in the Rhondda, and the smiling ever-welcome Princess in burgundy velvet with a feathered hat was another sensation. Children besieged her, and for some, who burst into tears when she spoke to them, it was all too much. But she was ready with a word of comfort and a tweak to a child's hat, and they loved her for it. There were more presentations including official ones of armchairs in Welsh leather and a black Welsh heifer and ewe which they duly admired. They toured a hospital, giving special delight to the mothers in a maternity hospital, the Prince telling one proud mother of a child born that day she 'ought to be asleep'.

And so to Cardiff where they were entertained with a display of gymnastics by children between the ages of five and twelve, and then had a chance to meet the people.

In the evening, in a blue chiffon dress, the Princess of Wales was sworn in as the 53rd Freeman of the City of Cardiff and was presented with a silver casket containing the Freedom scroll by the Lord Mayor, the second woman to have been so honoured in the City's history.

Then, to the delight of everyone, the Princess replied in Welsh, expressing her thanks and that 'she would love to come again soon'. There was a standing ovation from the audience, and the Princess told them she was proud to be the Princess of Wales. Prince Charles had himself received the Freedom of the City in 1969 after his Investiture.

The first visit to Wales by the new Princess of Wales was an outstanding success, and at times she must have felt moved by the immensity of her welcome from the people. The Prince, always conscious of the affection with which he is held in Wales, must have been very proud of his Princess and the way in which she quickly endeared herself to the Welsh people. Her charm and beauty and the spontaneity of her smile won her many

The rain could not deter anyone from feeling happy.

Above: The Princess surrounded by delighted Welsh people all anxious to meet her.

Right: The Princess of Wales receives the casket containing the Freedom Scroll granting her the Freedom of the City of Cardiff.

164

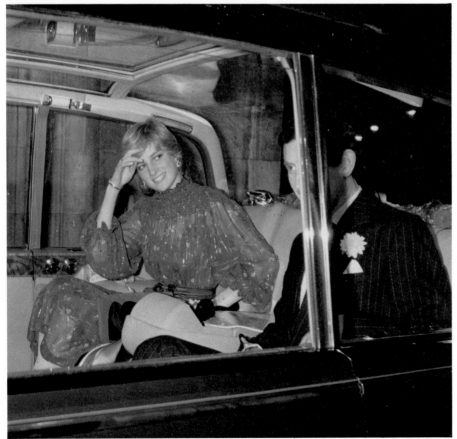

Above: Hands reach to touch her as the Princess tours Brecon.

Left: The Prince and Princess leaving Cardiff City Hall after she had been made a Freeman of the City.

hearts, and already they are looking forward with pleasure to the next visit.

In London at the beginning of November, the Prince and Princess of Wales opened the twenty-fifth London Film Festival at the National Film Theatre on the South Bank. Once again the Princess set a fashion note with her black velvet dress and Elizabethan collar. She smilingly acknowledged the cheers of those who had gathered to catch a glimpse of her.

Wednesday, 4 November, was a day of splendour, the occasion of the State Opening of Parliament by the Queen. As the Princess climbed into the glass coach that was to take her to the ceremony, she must have been reminded of an earlier journey in the same coach in July, for it was the one that had taken her to her wedding at St Paul's Cathedral. There was the traditional pomp and pageantry, with the clinking of horse trappings as the escort rode beside the coach bearing Prince Charles and his wife with Princess Anne and her husband Captain Mark Phillips to the Palace of Westminster.

Four-year-old Alexandra Spencer-Churchill, daughter of the Duke and Duchess of Marlborough, presenting a bouquet to the Princess of Wales when she and the Prince visited Blenheim Palace for a performance by the English Chamber Orchestra.

166

Above and left: The Princess, in a becoming black dress with a white lace collar, accompanies her husband to the National Film Theatre to open the London Film Festival.

167

The Princess, in a beautiful white dress and tiara, sits beside Prince Charles in the House of Lords while attending her first State Opening of Parliament. On the other side of the enthroned Queen and the Duke of Edinburgh are Princess Anne and Captain Mark Phillips.

With Princess Anne at her side the Princess rides in the Glass Coach once more to attend the State Opening of Parliament.

Opposite page: The Princess of Wales in a beautiful dress at the Victoria and Albert Museum's 'Splendours of the Gonzaga' exhibition.

It was the first time in seventy years that a Princess of Wales had attended the State Opening of Parliament, and this Princess looked radiant. She was wearing a simple white and silver gauze dress and tiara, stark in its simplicity compared with the richer dresses of the Queen and Princess Anne. Seated by her husband on the right of the Queen, the Princess listened attentively to the Queen's Speech and then returned once more in procession to Buckingham Palace.

For the first time in the ceremony, the Cap of Maintenance was held by Baroness Young, the first woman ever to do so.

In the evening the Prince and Princess inaugurated the exhibition 'Splendours of the Gonzaga' at the Victoria and Albert Museum, of which the Prince is the patron. Nearly three hundred paintings, drawings, prints, sculpture, furniture, ceramics and other items bring to life the world of the Gonzaga in one of the most imaginative exhibitions ever held.

On 5 November there came a surprise and very welcome announcement from Buckingham Palace at 11 am. The simple message was very clear: 'The Princess of Wales is expecting a baby next June.' And the statement added, 'The Prince and Princess of Wales, the Queen and the Duke of Edinburgh and members of both families are delighted by the news'.

The Queen had been personally informed of the news by the Prince and Princess some days before, and the Princess's mother and father were also 'absolutely delighted'.

170

It was announced that 'The Princess is in excellent health. She hopes to continue to undertake some public engagements but regrets the disappointment which may be caused by any curtailment in her planned programme.' The tour of Australia, New Zealand and Canada planned for 1982 was cancelled, but there was general rejoicing throughout the Commonwealth.

Two hours after the news of the baby had been announced the happily smiling Prince and Princess of Wales were the guests of the Lord Mayor and City of London at Guildhall for luncheon. The Lord Mayor told the six hundred guests that the City rejoiced, and the Prince responded, while his wife smiled shyly at the enthusiasm. Outside there were special cheers, for by now everyone had heard the news and wanted to show their pleasure. Messages of love and congratulations poured in to Buckingham Palace, and there were special celebrations at Tetbury, near their home at Highgrove.

The Prince of Wales acknowledges the good wishes of the City of London at a luncheon at Guildhall given by the Lord Mayor. The Princess looks on.

The exciting week had a sobering end. The Prince and Princess, with other members of the Royal Family, attended the Royal British Legion Sixtieth Annual Festival of Remembrance for the dead of two world wars at the Royal Albert Hall. The military bands played a light-hearted tribute with 'Congratulations' during the evening.

The Princess of Wales watching the Remembrance Day service at the Cenotaph in Whitehall, with King Olaf of Norway, Princess Alice Duchess of Gloucester and the Queen Mother.

In an open Land-Rover the Prince and Princess are driven round the stadium at York to the delight of cheering crowds.

173

A smiling Princess at the National Railway Museum in York.

On the balcony, the Prince and Princess acknowledge the cheers of Chesterfield.

The Princess smilingly accepts a plastic duck for her baby from a wellwisher at Chesterfield.

Next morning, the Princess with the Queen Mother and other members of the Family watched from a balcony in Whitehall as the Queen, Prince Philip, Prince Charles and others laid their wreaths on the Cenotaph and took part in the annual religious service.

Unfortunately, the Princess had to cancel some of her engagements as she was feeling unwell, but was able to accompany Prince Charles on a visit to York.

Here they rode in an open carriage and were showered with gifts of all kinds from cuddly toys and baby clothes to about a thousand posies and flowers as they went on an informal walkabout in the streets of the city. They had visited the National Railway Museum, and the Prince had had a ride on different trains watched by his wife. In the City Stadium they were cheered by seven thousand schoolchildren on the terraces, and the Prince piloted the helicopter taking the royal couple on to another engagement at Chesterfield, where they opened a shopping precinct and police headquarters. Wellwishers were much in evidence, and the smiling Prince and Princess were the recipients of hundreds of toys, clothes, flowers and other gifts.

175

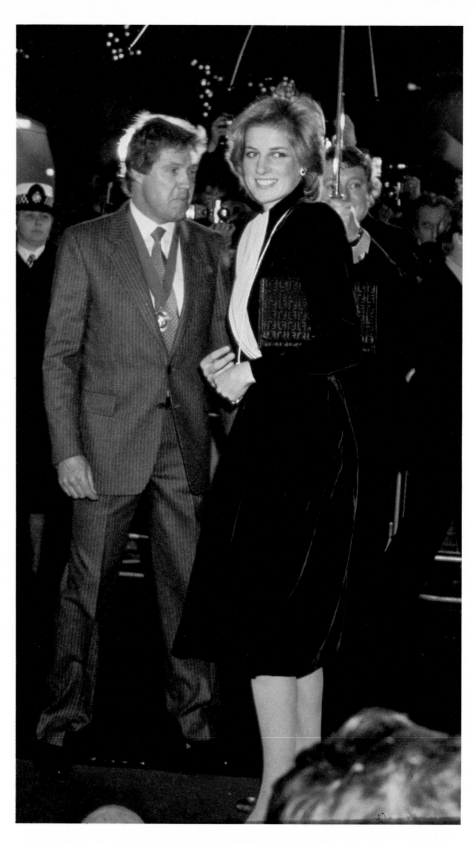

At her first solo engagement the Princess switches on the lights in Regent Street for the 1981 Christmas decorations.

A few days later it was time for the Princess to perform her first solo engagement. Dressed in a midnight blue velvet suit trimmed with silver piping, she stepped out on to a balcony in London's Regent Street. There she made a short speech saying how delighted she was to contribute to the festive spirit in London, and then, amid cheers, she switched on the Christmas lights. The whole of Regent Street was ablaze with the lights of the huge Christmas trees bedecked with presents which were the special decorations for this Christmas of 1981.

176

The First Christmas

The last weeks of 1981 were busy ones for the Princess of Wales. Prince Charles and his bride were settling into Highgrove, their first country house. Like any other couple in their first home they had much to deal with, the arrangement of their presents and furniture and the adjustment to a new life. There was also a varied programme of private and official engagements to carry out.

An informal lunch at the Royal Yacht Club in London was preceded by a light-hearted tree-planting ceremony. The Princess planted three flowering cherries, two to commemorate the Royal Wedding and a third in honour of the royal baby. Prince Charles planted three more cherry trees in a special copse in memory of his great-uncle, Lord Louis Mountbatten, a former Commodore of the Royal Yacht Club.

Below left: Prince Charles gives his wife a helping hand to plant some flowering cherry trees in Hyde Park on 20 November.

Below: Looking relaxed and happy in her red and black suit, the Princess uses a specially engraved silver spade for the commemorative tree-planting which was organized by the Royal Thames Yacht Club.

Opposite page: At the tree-planting ceremony in Hyde Park the Princess was presented with this beautiful bouquet.

Above: Wearing a green tweed suit and pink silk blouse, the Princess of Wales performed her second solo engagement when she opened the new head Post Office at Northampton.

Right: Her Royal Highness at the controls of some of the Post Office's most up-to-date machinery.

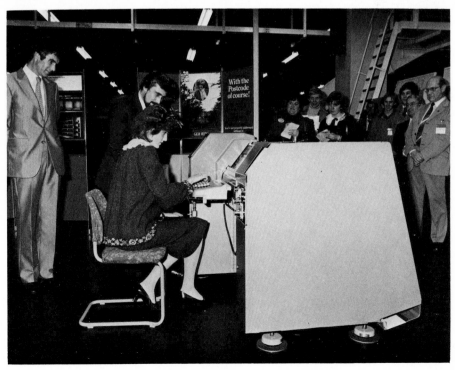

Right: The Princess seen leaving a shop in Tetbury clutching in her hands the goods she had just purchased. Her detective, who is just behind her, helped out when she had insufficient money in her purse to pay for them!

The Princess, with Prince Andrew in the background, talking to members of the Royal Opera House before the performance of the ballet Romeo and Juliet *on 25 November.*

The Princess shares her husband's love of music and art, and their visit to the Royal Opera House, Covent Garden, to attend a performance of *Romeo and Juliet* in celebration of their marriage was by invitation of the Board of Directors. Their second and third visits were private ones to hear the operas *Tosca* and *Il Trovatore*, and in mid December they attended the Friends of Covent Garden Christmas Party.

Cool December lived up to its name with blizzard conditions in many areas, but began with a warm occasion, dinner with the Speaker and Members of the House of Commons. The Right Hon. George Thomas, who read the Lesson at the Royal Wedding and participated in Prince Charles's Investiture, had been keenly involved, as a Welshman, in their recent visit to the Principality.

The BBC gave a private showing of an edited one hundred minutes of the film of the Royal Wedding for the staff, grooms, footmen and others who were actually taking part and had therefore been unable to see it on the day. The rest of the nation had a second chance on 13 December when they were able to relive the momentous occasion. For many the sight of sunshine was very welcome as the country was gripped in arctic conditions with deep blizzards everywhere.

The Prince and Princess, together with Prince Philip, were among the members of the Royal Family who paid a short visit to Balmoral. Once again the antics of their dogs when alighting from the aircraft afforded much amusement for the photographers on their return.

Already the Prince and Princess of Wales are familiar figures on the Tetbury scene where they are welcomed by local residents as part of the community and can move about freely. The new pair of gates at

Above: The Queen and Prince Philip entertained the EEC heads of government to luncheon at Buckingham Palace on 26 November on the occasion of their talks in London. The Prince and Princess of Wales were among the guests and are seen in the formal photograph that was taken to mark the event.

Left: On the evening of 1 December Prince Charles and his wife were entertained to dinner at the House of Commons by the Speaker, the Right Hon. George Thomas, and posed for this photograph with their host.

On 6 December the Prince and Princess attended a concert in aid of the Benjamin Britten Foundation at Tetbury Church in Gloucestershire, and are seen being greeted by local dignitaries on their arrival.

The Princess of Wales's unforgettable wedding dress, flanked by a bridesmaid's dress and a page's uniform, makes a striking centrepiece for a touring exhibition of two hundred of the wedding presents given to the royal couple in July.

Highgrove that Tetbury residents had given them as a wedding present were on exhibition in the Town Hall in December before being delivered to the house for hanging. When possible the royal couple attend functions in Tetbury and on 6 December they went to a concert in aid of the Benjamin Britten Foundation (which aids young musicians) at St Mary's Church. Afterwards the Princess was presented with a porcelain copy of her wedding bouquet.

A touring exhibition of the Princess of Wales's wedding dress, a bridesmaid's dress and a page's uniform, with a selection of about two hundred of the wedding presents opened at Cardiff Castle on 10 December. The exhibition went on to Edinburgh in late January and to other centres, giving many more people a chance to see for themselves, and add to the sum of more than £80,000 already raised for the disabled when the collection of presents and dresses was on show at St James's Palace in London.

In February when the royal engagement was announced the children of St Mary's School at Tetbury had written to the Princess, and later in the year a visit was arranged for December. On a very snowy day the Princess arrived, driving herself from Highgrove in her silver Ford Escort, complete with Kermit the frog mascot, seemingly unperturbed by the weather. The children gave her a rapturous welcome. It was early morning so the Princess sat with the pupils for morning assembly. A sign welcomed her in Welsh and she joined in the carols before going on a tour

On a cold, snowy day in early December the Princess paid a private visit to the children at St Mary's Church of England Junior School at Tetbury. During her two-hour stay the Princess sang carols and toured the school, showing a keen interest in the decorations and paintings made for her by the children.

of the school. The classrooms had been carefully decorated and there were Christmas trees and a special nativity scene. For two hours the children enjoyed her company and she took a keen interest in all their activities. The Princess was presented with an inscribed glass paperweight engraved with the Prince of Wales's feathers. To more cheers the Princess drove home, promising to come and see them all again soon.

The winter snow lay very crisp as, wearing a Cossack-style hat in fur with muff to match and high boots, the Princess arrived with her husband to attend a service at Gloucester Cathedral. The cathedral was celebrating its 1300th anniversary in 1981.

A week later the Prince and Princess visited another cathedral, this time the modern one at Guildford where there was a Christmas celebration in aid of the Prince's Trust, of which he is President. Afterwards, despite the snow and cold, the Prince and Princess had one of their popular walkabouts, meeting many of the youngsters who took part in the service.

Next day they were in London fulfilling a final pre-Christmas engagement to visit the Manor of Kennington as Duke and Duchess of Cornwall.

And so to Christmas itself. Traditionally, the Royal Family always go to Windsor for the celebrations, with the Castle taking on a new look as decorations lighten its grey walls. There is a Christmas tree and everyone takes part in its decoration and the placing of gifts around it.

The Christmas holiday at Windsor is a family time when all members gather for the festivities. Two of them celebrate their birthdays on Christmas Day. Princess Alice, Dowager Duchess of Gloucester, was eighty. Her three grandchildren are a great source of delight, and through her Danish daughter-in-law, the Duchess of Gloucester, she has learnt new Christmas traditions from Scandinavia. The second to celebrate her

The Princess smiles through the snowflakes as she arrives with Prince Charles to attend a Christmas celebration in Guildford Cathedral on 21 December. Afterwards she met many of those who had waited outside in the snow to catch a glimpse of her.

birthday was 45-year-old Princess Alexandra, wife of the Hon. Angus Ogilvy and one of the most popular members of the family.

Nowadays the Royal Family is so large that in some ways the Christmas party was like those held in Queen Victoria's time, and the Princess of Wales had ample opportunity to entertain her favourite under-five age group. The family has members in every age group from the Queen Mother in her eighties to Princess Alexandra's teenage children, the toddling infants of the Duke and Duchess of Gloucester and Prince and Princess Michael, and the baby daughters of Princess Anne and Princess Michael born in 1981. The Queen's younger sons and Princess Margaret's children are next in age to the married grown-ups, so there are players for every game and the pattern is similar over the years.

On Christmas Eve the family arrives and they exchange presents. The huge Christmas tree comes from the royal estates, and the Queen switches on its lights before giving out the gifts. The children have theirs on Christmas Day and, like children the world over, have the pleasure of traditional stockings.

Christmas morning is very special. The Royal Family attend Morning Service in St George's Chapel at Windsor, and afterwards talk informally as they descend the wide steps to their cars. This year there was a particular

Above: The Princess stooping to talk to children who had taken part in a Nativity play during the royal couple's visit to Guildford Cathedral.

Left: The Prince and Princess talking to church dignitaries and others who had taken part in the Christmas celebrations at Guildford Cathedral.

Overleaf: The now traditional Christmas Day picture of the Royal Family descending the steps of St George's Chapel, Windsor, after attending Morning Service. The Queen is seen talking to the Dean of Windsor, and the Princess of Wales (at her first Royal Christmas Day Service) is on the left, talking to Prince Edward.

welcome for the Princess of Wales, warmly wrapped in a blue coat.

Back at the Castle the royal festivities are similar to those enjoyed by many of the Queen's subjects. The turkeys come from one of the royal farms, and the recipe for the plum pudding has been handed down for many generations.

During the last war one of the highlights was the Christmas pantomime in which the Queen and Princess Margaret were the stars, and the royal children of today are no less talented. An informal dance, party games and music add to the entertainment.

The Queen gives presents to all her employees in the royal homes and on the royal yacht, and trees from Sandringham are given to schools in the area. Queen Victoria sent bags of coal to the needy in Windsor in her time.

The Queen's Christmas Day television broadcast, which is recorded in advance, referred to 1981 as the International Year of Disabled People and showed on screen a recent occasion at Buckingham Palace when the Queen, with the Prince and Princess of Wales, met and took a keen interest in many disabled people who had come to receive new cars. The Princess smilingly asked one owner who would clean the car and the Prince sympathized with another who had had problems with the driving test. The Princess's innate sympathy and understanding were very marked, and in the Year of Disabled People both the Prince (who is Patron) and his wife have worked caringly for this cause. It was, indeed, to work with the disabled that the proceeds from sales of the official wedding souvenir and programme went.

On 28 December the *Today* programme on Radio 4 announced that its listeners had voted the Princess of Wales female personality of the year for 1981. Prince Charles is the male personality.

Three days after Christmas the royal party went their separate ways. Prince Philip with Princes Andrew and Edward went to Sandringham, followed by the Prince and Princess of Wales who came after lunch. Crowds waited in the cold to greet them by the main entrance, but they

A close-up of the Prince and Princess of Wales as they wait for their car on the steps of St George's Chapel. Accompanying them is the Dean of Windsor who officiated at the Christmas Day Service.

The Princess's elegant blue maternity coat is shown to advantage as she and the Prince pause for a moment before leaving St George's Chapel to enjoy the Christmas festivities at Windsor Castle.

slipped in by another gate. The Queen and the Queen Mother arrived by tea time and the annual holiday in Norfolk had begun.

In the New Year Honours List Police Superintendent Paul Officer, Prince Charles's bodyguard for twelve years before being temporarily bodyguard to the Princess, received a personal honour from the Queen. He became a member of the Royal Victorian Order, and is now performing other police duties.

For the Princess of Wales the New Year in Norfolk had a twofold significance. It was a time of new beginning, a looking forward to the future and all that 1982 would bring. The joy of her first child in June would be another milestone, her 21st birthday in July and first wedding anniversary days to celebrate.

Equally significantly Sandringham, the place where her life had begun at Park House, was a place for memories. During the family holiday the Princess could walk again the broad acres of the estate, perhaps explore long-forgotten childhood places of enchantment. With Prince Charles at her side, she would surely discover new delights to savour in the months that lay ahead.

The years had come full circle. The little girl who had played in the snow and the summer pasture long ago had returned the third lady in the land. It was with her own family that her story had begun but it was as a member of the Royal Family that she would begin the new year ahead.

Acknowledgments

The photographs on pages 10 top and 152 top are reproduced by Gracious Permission of Her Majesty The Queen. The photograph on page 72 is from the joint ITV/BBC programme by courtesy of Thames Television.

Associated Newspapers, London 44, 49 bottom, 76, 77 top, 77 bottom left, 77 bottom right, 78 top, 79 top left, 79 top right, 80 top, 80 bottom, 82 right, 90 top, 90 bottom right, 96 bottom, 98, 104 bottom, 109, 124 bottom, 144 top; Beedle & Cooper, Northampton 30-31; BIPNA, London 106, 113 bottom, 114, 115, 118, 123 bottom, 125, 129, 132 left, 132 right, 134 bottom left; BBC Hulton Picture Library, London 7, 10 bottom, 13 top left, 15 top right, 149 top, 149 bottom, 150, 151; Camera Press, London – Lionel Cherruault 42 left, 65, 157, 160, 177 left, 190, 191, Tony Drabble 55 top, 61 top, ILN 110-111, Andy Kyle 170, Patrick Lichfield 128 bottom, 130, 131, LNS 47, Richard Slade 103, 104 top, Les Wilson 26; Central Press, London 11, 12, 13 bottom, 16 left, 16 right, 17, 41, 56 bottom, 57 top, 57 bottom, 78 bottom, 81 bottom, 85, 88-89, 90 bottom left, 94, 95 top, 152 bottom, 153, 172, 173 bottom, 181 bottom; Eastern Counties Newspapers, Norwich 20, 23; Epoque, London 84, 86 top; Fox Photos, London 74-75, 179 top, 179 bottom, 181 top, 187 top, 187 bottom, 188-189; Tim Graham, London 6, 27, 33 top, 37, 40 top, 40 bottom, 42 right, 43, 45, 48, 49 top, 50 top, 52 top right, 52 bottom, 54, 58 right, 60 top, 60 bottom, 66, 69, 70 top, 81 top, 96 top, 97 top, 99, 100, 107, 112, 113 top, 119, 120, 122, 123 top, 124 top, 135, 136-137, 138 bottom, 141, 142 bottom right, 146, 147 top, 155, 156, 158-159, 161 top, 161 bottom, 162, 163, 165 top, 165 bottom, 171, 173 top, 175, 178, 183, 185; Mitch Jenkins, Northampton 32 bottom; Mansell Collection, London 15 bottom, 147 bottom; National Portrait Gallery, London 13 top right, 14; Northampton Mercury 15 top left, 22 bottom, 28, 34 left, 73 top right; Photographers International, Chilworth 25 bottom, 34 right, 39, 50 bottom right, 62-63, 70 bottom, 134 top, 138 top, 140 bottom, 142 top, 174 bottom, 176; Popperfoto, London 148 bottom right; Press Association, London 18, 19, 21 top, 21 bottom, 24 right, 32 top, 51, 58 left, 71, 73 top left, 108, 133, 144 bottom, 145 bottom, 148 top, 148 centre, 148 bottom left, 154 bottom, 164 bottom, 166, 168-169, 174 top, 180 bottom, 184, 186; Rex Features, London 29, 35 bottom, 36, 38, 46 top, 50 bottom left, 56 top, 67, 68 top, 73 bottom, 83, 86 bottom, 87, 95 bottom, 101, 102, 105 top, 105 bottom, 116, 117 bottom, 121, 126-127, 134 bottom right, 139 top, 143, 145 top, 164 top, 167 top, 167 bottom; Syndication International, London 22 top, 24 left, 25 top, 33 bottom, 35 top, 46 bottom, 52 top left, 53 top, 53 centre, 53 bottom, 55 bottom, 59, 61 bottom, 64, 68 bottom, 79 bottom, 82 left, 91, 92, 93 top, 93 bottom, 97 bottom, 117 top, 128 top, 139 bottom, 140 top, 142 bottom left, 154 top, 177 right, 180 top, 182 top, 182 bottom; Tony Taylor, Headley Down 8-9.

Front cover: Camera Press, London – Snowdon.
Back cover: Tim Graham, London.
Frontispiece: Tim Graham, London.